PRESENTING
AUSTRALIA

PRESENTING AUSTRALIA

THE MAKING OF A NATION

BRUCE ELDER

First published in Australia in 2000
by New Holland Publishers (Australia) Pty Ltd
Sydney • Auckland • London • Cape Town

Produced and published in Australia
by New Holland Publishers (Australia) Pty Ltd
14 Aquatic Drive Frenchs Forest NSW 2086 Australia
218 Lake Road Northcote Auckland New Zealand
24 Nutford Place London W1H 6DQ United Kingdom
80 McKenzie Street Cape Town 8001 South Africa

National Library of Australia
Cataloguing-in-Publication data:

Elder, Bruce.
Presenting Australia – The Making of a Nation.

Includes index
ISBN 1 86436 527 7.

1. Australia - History - Pictorial works. 2. Australia - History.
3. Australia - Pictorial works. I. Title.

994

Publishing Manager: Anouska Good
Project Editor: Monica Ban
Copy Editor: Karen Enkelaar
Designer: Nanette Backhouse
Picture Researcher: Kirsti Wright
Artwork: Jeff Lang Illustration
Reproduction: Colour Scan
Printer: South China Printing

PHOTOGRAPHIC ACKNOWLEDGEMENTS

NHIL: New Holland Image Library
APL: Australian Picture Library
PLA: Photo Library of Australia

Paul Sinclair: Front Cover, p15, 18, 68, 179 **John Meier:** p1, 2–3, 6, 8, 9, 11, 64, 70–71, 78–79, 88–89, 90, 91, 92, 93, 130, 132–133, 168 **Stuart Owen Fox:** p10, 28 (right), 94–95, 100, 101, 104–105, 106, 115, 131, 140–141, 153, 172–173, 178, 181 **Ted Mead:** p12, 24, 25, 27, 29 (left), 108–109, 118–119, 123, 124–125, 138, 139, 147, 164–165, 171, 184–185, 187 **Richard I'Anson:** p14, 31 (left), 74, 77, 103, 114, 150–151, 156–157, 166, 169, 186, 189 **Nick Rains:** p22 (right), 180 **Joe Shemesh:** p134 **Don Fuchs:** 29 (right), 30 (left), 57 (bottom left), 75, 76 **Grant Murray:** p116 **APL/Nick Rains:** p22 (left) **Coo-ee Picture Library:** p51, 57 (top & bottom right), 66, 82, 112, 113, 144 **National Library of Australia:** pp4–5, 30 (right), 31 (right), 32, 33, 34, 35, 36, 37, 38, 39, 40, 41, 42, 43, 44, 45, 46, 47, 49, 50, 53 (right), 54, 55, 60, 61, 62, 63, 80, 83, 96, 98, 99, 110, 111, 126, 127, 128, 129, 142, 143, 145, 146, 158, 159, 160, 161, 174, 175, 176, 177, Back Cover insets **La Trobe Collection/State Library of Victoria:** p48, 52, 53 (left), 81, 85 (right) **Tony Karacsonyi:** p28 (left) **PLA/Roberto Matassa:** p56 **PLA/David Messent:** pp58–59 **PLA/Neil   Duncan:** p67 **PLA/Ken Stepnell:** p85, 149 **PLA/Kurt Vollmer:** p107 **PLA/Richard Woldendorp:** p122, 162 **PLA/Ted Mead:** p137 **PLA/Robin Smith:** p148 **PLA/Paul Nevin:** p152 **PLA/David Roche:** p154 **PLA/Col Roberts:** p170 **PLA/Alain Evrard:** p183 **PLA/Stefan Mokrzecki:** p188 **NHIL:** p27, 120, 182, Back Cover **NHIL/Shaen Adey:** p65, 84, 121 **NHIL/Anthony Johnson:** p102, 167 **Courtesy of Peter Luck:** p69

CONTENTS

NEW SOUTH WALES

THE PREMIER STATE

VICTORIA

THE GARDEN STATE

Australian Capital Territory

THE FEDERAL CAPITAL

QUEENSLAND

THE SUNSHINE STATE

Tasmania

THE APPLE ISLE

SOUTH AUSTRALIA

THE FESTIVAL STATE

WESTERN AUSTRALIA

THE WILDFLOWER STATE

NORTHERN TERRITORY

THE TOP END

TIMOR

SEA

ARAFUR

Melville
Island

Bathurst
Island

DARWIN

Kakadu NP

ARNH
LAN

Litchfield NP

Nitmiluk
(Katherine G

Drysdale
River NP

Kununurra

*KIMBERLEY
REGION*

Gregory NP

KING
LEOPOLD RANGE

DURACK RANGE

Lake
Argyle

NORTHER

TERRITOR

Purnululu
(Bungle Bungle)
NP

Broome

BUNGLE BUNGLE
RANGE

TANAMI DESERT

STUART HIGHWAY

BA

GREAT NORTHERN HIGHWAY

*Tennant
Creek*

Devils Marbles

DAVENP

Dampier

Port Hedland

Millstream–
Chichester NP

Lake
Mackay

Ningaloo
Marine Park

Karijini
(Hamersley Range)
NP

GIBSON DESERT

Alice Springs

West MacDonnell NP

HAMERSLEY RANGE

Lake
Disappointment

Lake
Neale

Finke Gorge NP

Kings Canyon

MACDON

RANG

Lake
MacLeod

PETERMANN RANGES

Uluru–Kata Tjuta NP

Carnarvon

LITTLE SANDY DESERT

Shark Bay

Dirk Hartog
Island

WESTERN
AUSTRALIA

SOUTH

AUSTRALI

Kalbarri NP

GREAT VICTORIA DESERT

Coober Pedy

GREAT NORTHERN HIGHWAY

Houtman
Abrolhos

Geraldton

Nambung NP

NULLARBOR PLAIN

EYRE HIGHWA

GREAT EASTERN HIGHWAY

PERTH
Fremantle

Wave Rock

Norseman

GREAT AUSTRALIAN BIGHT

Rottnest Island

DARLING RANGE

Cape Arid NP

Leeuwin–
Naturaliste NP

Stirling Range NP

Fitzgerald
River NP

Cape Le
Grande NP

Albany

INDIAN OCEAN

SOUTHERN

OCEAN

N

TORRES STRAIT

Thursday
Island · Cape York

Jardine River
NP

CAPE
YORK
PENINSULA

GULF OF

CARPENTARIA

Lakefield
NP

Cooktown

Cape Tribulation
NP

Daintree NP

Cairns

ATHERTON TABLELAND

Hinchinbrook Island

CORAL SEA

Lawn
Hill NP

Townsville

Mount Isa

FLINDERS HIGHWAY

Airlie Beach

Whitsunday Islands

QUEENSLAND

GREAT BARRIER REEF

Diamantina
NP

Rockhampton

Simpson
Desert
NP

Carnarvon NP

Lake Machattie

Great Sandy NP

Fraser Island

STURTS STONY
DESERT

Noosa

Glasshouse Mountains

Lake Eyre

Lake Eyre NP

BRISBANE

Lamington NP

Strzelecki
Regional
Reserve

Sturt NP

STRZELECKI
DESERT

Byron Bay

Lake
Torrens

NEW
SOUTH
WALES

Mootwingee NP

Lake
Frome

Dorrigo NP

Coffs Harbour

FLINDERS RANGES

Broken
Hill

Darling River

Barrington
Tops NP

Port
Lincoln

Mungo NP

Bathurst

Wollemi
NP

Newcastle

Blue Mountains NP

SYDNEY

ADELAIDE

Murrumbidgee River

A.C.T.

Wollongong

Murray–
Sunset NP

CANBERRA

Coorong
NP

Wyperfeld
NP

Murray River

Lake
Jindabyne

Kangaroo
Island

VICTORIA

Lake
Eucumbene

Grampians
(Gariwerd) NP

Bendigo

Mt Buffalo NP

Alpine NP

Ben Boyd NP

Mount Gambier

Ballarat

MELBOURNE

Geelong

Croajingolong NP

Snowy River NP

Port
Campbell
NP

Wilsons
Promontory NP

BASS STRAIT

Flinders
Island

TASMANIA

Launceston

Cradle Mtn–
Lake St Clair NP

Freycinet NP

Franklin–Gordon
Wild Rivers NP

HOBART

Port Arthur

Southwest NP

GREAT DIVIDING RANGE

SOUTH PACIFIC OCEAN

TASMAN

SEA

SCALE

500 km

INTRODUCTION

THE LUCKY COUNTRY

Australia is a series of complex contradictions. It seems to be at once the oldest and the youngest continent in the world—old in the sense that some of its rock outcrops are over 1200 million years old, and young in the sense that Tasmania was separated from the mainland as recently as 6000 years ago. Australia has boasted continuous human settlement for at least 60 000 years (perhaps, according to some theorists, even 120 000 years), yet it established its unique geopolitical identity as a modern country only as recently as 1901.

It is both a 'lucky country' and an 'unlucky country'. On the one hand it has vast natural resources yet it contains the world's third-largest desert area (after the Sahara and Antarctica), and it is locked in the contradiction that it is a predominantly European country sitting uncertainly on the edge of Asia.

It is a country with a history which, on the surface, seems deceptively simple and yet, as historians slowly uncover the truth, this impression is giving way to something far more tragic and complicated. (It is remarkable that, only as recently as the 1980s and 1990s, the history of the country has been referred to as 'discovery–settlement–exploration–gold–federation–nationhood–national identity'.)

Above and opposite: Australia is the most ancient of all the continents where rocks, over thousands of millions of years, have been twisted and eroded into patterns of great natural beauty.

Above: Marble Bar in Western Australia was named after a unique and beautiful bar of jasper (a highly coloured cryptocrystalline variety of quartz) which crosses the Coongan River west of the town.

THE LAND

Australia is an ancient continent. Geologists have found rocks which they estimate are 4500 million years old. It was originally part of a vast southern landmass known as Gondwana. About 100 million years ago, Gondwana separated from Antarctica and moved northwards. Twenty million years later, the island groups of Australasia, notably New Zealand and New Caledonia, split from the larger continent.

For 80 million years, with little mountain building occurring, the land was eroded so that Australia is now the flattest and lowest continent on Earth. The result is that Mount Kosciuszko, the continent's highest mountain, is only 2228 metres above sea level, and the rocky outcrops of central Australia were mountain ranges now reduced to small hills. Uluru is a remnant of an eroded mountain range. Similarly, the MacDonnell Ranges near Alice Springs are so weathered they are like the exposed bare bones of the Earth.

Continental Australia can be divided into three major geological areas. The western plateau has existed as a landmass for over 500 million years and has some of the oldest rocks on Earth. It stretches from the coast of Western Australia to outback Queensland and includes the vast Great Sandy, Gibson and Great Victoria deserts as well as the ancient plateaux in the Kimberleys, Arnhem Land and the Hamersley Ranges.

The central lowlands run south from the Gulf of Carpentaria to Victoria and South Australia and include the Murray-Darling plains and the Great Artesian Basin. They are flat, inhospitable and marginal lands characterised by eroded mountain ranges, vast salt lakes, sand dunes and extensive sedimentary deposits.

Rising from the central lowlands are the eastern highlands—a series of plateaux and low mountain ranges which run the length of the eastern coast of Australia. The most prominent of these is the Great Dividing Range, characterised by waterfalls and rivers which flow west to the centre of the continent.

The eastern highlands drop to a coastal plain where rocky headlands, beautiful sandy beaches, extensive coastal wetlands and rich, fertile coastal plains are watered by the short rivers which begin in the highlands. The coastal region is where most of Australia's population lives. It is the agricultural heartland of the country. The lowlands are ideal dairy and beef cattle country and the coastal plains grow a variety of crops from sugar cane to pineapples and bananas.

Above: Blood-red desert soils greet the traveller who gazes on the mesas and rocky outcrops. This is Pyramid Hill in the Pilbara's Chichester Range.

Above left: Australia has the second largest hot desert area in the world—after the Sahara. The inland, at places like Moomba in South Australia, has sand dunes which stretch to the horizon.

Above right: Hot days and heavy rainfall ensure that much of the coastal strip of Queensland and northern New South Wales is fertile and productive.

THE CLIMATE

Australia is marked by great climatic variation. Its size (7 682 300 square kilometres) and latitudinal range (10°41´S to 43°39´S) produce climates which range from hot and steamy tropics to deserts with great daily temperature extremes.

The tropics sprawl across the north of the continent and give way to sub-tropical and temperate conditions along the eastern coast. The Snowy Mountains in southern New South Wales and the highlands of Tasmania experience alpine conditions, but the vast majority of the continent—from the Western Australian coast across to south-west Queensland and north-west New South Wales—is arid desert.

Australia is a dry continent. More than half of the country receives less than 300 millimetres of rainfall per annum. This extreme dryness is increased by the dramatic effects of continentality. The centre of the continent is characterised by low levels of precipitation and temperature extremes. In Alice Springs it is common for the temperatures to soar above 35°C during the day and drop to below freezing during the night. The area between Oodnadatta in South Australia and Birdsville on the Queensland border receives an annual rainfall of less than 100 millimetres.

The desert region in Australia stretches from the Western Australian coast to the western regions of Queensland and New South Wales. The area is so dry that it is the world's second-largest hot desert area after the Sahara. The dryness of the continent is exacerbated by El Niño conditions—when there are abnormally warm surface waters in the tropical Pacific Ocean.

While the inland experiences temperatures over 40°C in summer, most of Australia experiences tropical and sub-tropical conditions: a mild, Mediterranean climate of wet winters and long, dry summers represent the populated areas of South and Western Australia; and balmy tropical winters and cyclonic summers typify the northern coasts of Queensland and Western Australia.

'The Wet' is the result of warm moist monsoonal air moving south from the equator and passing across northern Australia. The season is clearly defined. During September and October, the humidity begins to rise. In November, spectacular atmospheric displays of thunder and lightning occur and drenching monsoonal rains fill the rivers and wetlands.

Most of southern Australia experiences a Mediterranean-style climate. These conditions are ideal for growing crops such as wheat and are nearly perfect for the development of vineyards. Consequently, specific areas of South Australia and Western Australia are known for the quality of their wines and the richness of their wheat production.

Above left: Mountains hidden by clouds and mist and dense rainforests characterise most of the west coast of Tasmania.

Above right: Each winter snow covers the gum trees in the Snowy Mountains in both Victoria and New South Wales. These snowy branches are in the Mount Baw Baw National Park in northern Victoria.

Above: Generations of European Australians thought these strange grass trees looked like grass-skirted Aborigines carrying spears and named them 'black boys'. Today they are known as grass trees.

FLORA AND FAUNA

Australia's rich diversity of unique flora and fauna is a result of the continent being separated from other landmasses for over 40 million years. During that time plants and animals have evolved in isolation. They have survived in a diverse and non-competitive environment, which has resulted in Australia having over 25 000 species of plants.

Botanists believe this diversity is the result of the stability of the Australian continent's climate. This means that species were able to survive and evolve without being confronted by the dramatic changes in climate brought on by ice ages and periods of global warming.

In order to overcome infertile soils and infrequent rainfalls, Australian plants have developed their very own survival strategies to make clever use of their resources and take full advantage of the rare, but substantial, rainfall periods. The most obvious example of these plant survival mechanisms is the predominance—particularly in areas of desert,

Above: Kangaroo-paws (the floral emblem of Western Australia) bloom in the spring in the beautiful Stirling Range National Park.

Left: The rainforests of north Queensland abound in exotic tropical plants including these huge fan palms in the rainforest near Mission Beach.

heathland and mallee—of plants characterised by small sharp leaves such as banksias, bottlebrushes and tea-trees. Another example of Australian plants' survival is the long, slim shape of eucalypt leaves, which droop downwards, so that they minimise moisture loss during continuous hot, dry days.

As a consequence of its climate, Australia's natural vegetation (as opposed to the large number of recently imported species) is made up predominantly of giant eucalypts, scented acacias and hummock grasses.

There are around 500 species of eucalypt—both shrubs and trees—most of which are native to Australia. It has been estimated that there are more than 600 native varieties of acacia, and the *triodia* and *plectrachne* genera of the hummock grass are widespread from western Queensland through to the desert areas of the Northern Territory and Western Australia.

Historically, the nature of the Australian environment, and particularly the nature of Australian vegetation, has been affected by Aborigines who periodically set the bush alight. This action was undertaken for a number of reasons: for hunting, for signalling to other groups, to clear ground, to hold back the southern advance of the tropical rainforest, to kill vermin, and to regenerate plants which sustained both kangaroos and humans. Bush burning was not a haphazard process but rather a kind of farming. In fact, the term 'firestick farming' was coined in the late 1960s to describe the phenomenon.

Above: In August, the Australian bush changes from the drab grey of eucalypts to a magnificent yellow, when the wattle trees (Australia's national emblem) burst into bloom.

Right: In spring the marginal desert areas north of Perth are transformed by wildflower displays which blanket vast areas of the countryside.

Australian vegetation can be described as a combination of closed forests, open forests, woodlands, open woodlands, scrubs and heaths, shrublands, open shrublands and herblands. Closed forests exist in a small pocket on the west coast of Tasmania and in an extensive strip running north from Cairns. Open forests stretch down most of the east coast of the continent as well as the east coast of Tasmania and the south-western corner of Western Australia. Woodlands occur in a vast arc from the Northern Territory through to northern Queensland and down the east coast on and to the west of the Great Dividing Range.

Open woodlands and herblands once characterised the Queensland gulf country, while substantial areas of open woodlands existed in the southern Kimberley and to the north of the Nullarbor Plain. Shrublands stretched across the Nullarbor, existed in western Victoria and accounted for a huge area of central Western Australia, and open shrublands existed in what we now recognise as the desert areas of central Australia.

The settlement of the land by Europeans profoundly affected these divisions. The combined impact of timber cutters, graziers clearing the land, the extensive planting of

Above: The waratah, characterised by a globular head of bright red flowers, is the state flower of New South Wales.

Left: Fraser Island, the world's largest sand island, may have been produced by the Pacific Ocean but its lakes, like Lake Boomanjin seen here, are essentially pure, fresh water.

deciduous European trees and hoofed animals such as cows and sheep changed the vegetation of temperate Australia. In modern times, about 60 per cent of the continent is used for livestock grazing.

When it comes to the continent's native animals, its extraordinary stability and longevity has allowed many unique species to develop, adapt and survive. One of the widely accepted reasons for Australia's unique faunal diversity is the absence of seriously competitive predators—however, the continent once had and still does have predators. It once had the now extinct Tasmanian tiger (*Thylacinus cynocephalus*), the Tasmanian wolf and the marsupial lion (*Thylacoleo carnifex*), and fortunately still has the Tasmanian devil (*Sarcophilis harrisii*) and other predators ranging from dingoes and crocodiles to goannas. In recent times, there has been an increasing population of carnivorous feral dogs and cats.

There is also evidence of the presence of dinosaurs, particularly in far western Queensland. A plaque at the Dinosaur House in Hughenden explains the geographical origins of the area. One-hundred million years ago it was on the edge of a shallow inland sea that extended from what is now the Gulf of Carpentaria through to South Australia. Australia was then joined to Antarctica, but there were no polar ice caps and the world's climate was comparatively warm. Large marine reptiles called Icthyosaurus and Plesiosaurs swam in the inland sea, while land dinosaurs such as Muttaburrasaurus and the Austrosaurus browsed on the vegetation among conifers, cycads and ferns. Most of the remains of Muttaburrasaurus came from two individuals. The first was found in 1962 near Muttaburra,

Above: The kookaburra, sometimes called 'the laughing jackass', is known to all Australians because of its distinctive 'laughing' cry which echoes through the country's bushlands.

Right: The ubiquitous kangaroos in all their variety have spread across the Australian continent. Be warned: when annoyed they can be as mean as a heavyweight boxer.

from where it derives its name, and the other in 1987 near Hughenden. Their bones were preserved because the carcasses had been washed into the sea and became buried in the mud which protected them from total decay.

Similarly, 110 kilometres from Winton in western Queensland is the Lark Quarry Environmental Park with its famous Dinosaur Stampede which offers a fossilised insight into life some 95 million years ago. This is the largest group of footprints of running dinosaurs uncovered anywhere in the world. Three species of dinosaur made the 1200 tracks—a large flesh-eating carnosaur and many small coelurosaurs and ornithopods. Most of the footprints were made when a carnosaur trapped groups of coelurosaurs and ornithopods on the muddy edge of a lake.

Above: The dingo, a shy native dog, arrived on the Australian continent about 6000 years ago. It is one of the continent's few native predators.

Left: Living in the rivers of northern Australia the freshwater crocodile, seen here resting on the water's edge at Geike Gorge National Park in Western Australia, represents no threat to humans.

As far as can be determined, there were some 250 furred animals and 650 birds spread across the continent in 1788. Over millions of years these animals had modified themselves to survive in the harsh conditions of infertile soils, poor vegetation and intermittent droughts and floods. Their reproductive cycles were modified, their ability to use only limited supplies of protein, and their efficiency in making their young self-sufficient all contributed to species which, in many instances, were dramatically different from related species that had evolved on other continents.

There is evidence that a wide range of Australian animals—particularly mammals such as the koala, wombat and kangaroo as well as lizards and birds—reproduce sparingly. With small supplies of food available, nature compensates by limiting the animals' populations. The most extreme example of this is the mallee dragon lizard, whose adults die by the time their eggs hatch and a new generation arrives.

Although Australia is an island continent, and therefore has been less vulnerable to animal migration, it still has been affected by animals carried by birds and the winds, and by organisms floating across from the Indonesian archipelago. Since the arrival of humans, non-native animals have dramatically affected the continuing existence of a number of species. There is, for example, evidence that the arrival of dingoes led to the extinction of the flightless Tasmanian native hen on the mainland.

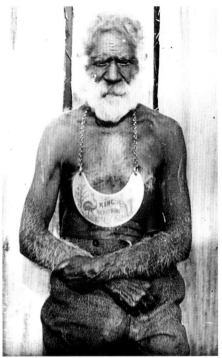

Above: The famous Lightning Man *painting at Nourlangie Rock in Kakadu National Park. This was repainted in 1964 by Barramundi Charlie of the Badmardi clan.*

Right: Although pre-European Aboriginal Australia had no kings or queens, the British insisted that tribal elders should wear metal plates indicating that they were Aboriginal 'royalty'.

FIRST INHABITANTS

Australia's original inhabitants probably arrived about 60 000 years ago, although it may have been as long ago as 120 000 years, and no-one knows with any certainty exactly where they came from. Some Aborigines insist that, according to the Dreamtime legends, they have always been here, that they came from nowhere and they have been here since the beginning of time. The western view is that the first Aborigines probably arrived having travelled across the Indonesian archipelago when the sea level around Australia was more than 120 metres lower than it is today. Certainly it can be assumed that they did not know the size or scale of the continent they had reached. In fact, at the time it is likely that mainland Australia, Tasmania and Papua New Guinea were all joined.

Over a period of 30 000 years, groups moved across the continent settling in areas of great richness such as the east coast and in areas of great hardship such as the dry, inhospitable Nullarbor Plain. As this settlement of the continent occurred, each group developed its own language, belief system, social system, art and culture.

Understanding of early Aboriginal settlement is constantly changing as pre-historians and archaeologists find new evidence of settlement. Tools found in the Swan River area of Western Australia are believed to date from around 38 000 years ago and provide evidence that Aborigines had reached the southern sectors of the continent at that time. Equally

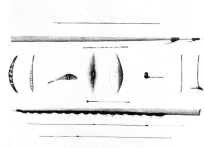

Above: Carefully cut and ground pieces of stone were used as arrows, axe heads and tips for spears by Aborigines.

Left: The main gallery at Ubirr in Kakadu National Park is renowned for its magnificent X-ray paintings of fish and other species.

important are the archaeological discoveries at Malangerr in the Northern Territory where stone axe heads dating back to 24 000 years ago have been found. These are some of the oldest axe heads found on Earth.

Discoveries at a number of other sites have given an indication of the spread of Aborigines throughout the Australian continent. Archaeologists have found evidence of stone tools at Keilor in Victoria that date back to 32 000 years ago, and in New South Wales, there is evidence that 26 000 years ago Aborigines were fishing for yabbies and other fresh-water life on the shores of Tandou Lake.

Archaeological finds suggest that 20 000 years ago most of the continent was inhabited and that Aborigines were actively using local resources in creative ways. There is evidence of settlement in Tasmania, at Mount Newman in Western Australia, in northern Queensland and in Arnhem Land. In these widely varying sites evidence has been found of flint mining, the use of ochre for artistic purposes, and the first finger painting on cave walls, such as that found on the walls of Koonalda Cave on the Nullarbor Plain.

Eight thousand years ago the narrow land corridor between Australia and New Guinea was cut off by the rising level of the ocean, and 6000 years ago, Tasmania had separated from the mainland, isolating the Aborigines living there. It was also around this time that the remarkable X-ray art found in the caves in Kakadu National Park, became a common feature of Aboriginal art.

Above: For 40 000 years Aborigines lived in ecological harmony with the land. Those who lived along the Murray River traded up and down the river and lived on fish.

EARLY SEAFARERS

No-one knows who were the first people to explore Australia after the Aborigines. The orthodoxy has always been that Europeans, particularly the great seafaring explorers from Portugal and Holland, were the first to sail along the coast but this conveniently ignores the fact that the Chinese probably arrived on the continent's north coast as early as the fifteenth century. Evidence suggests that the Chinese navigator, Cheng Ho, predates all his European competitors and a statue found near the present-day site of Darwin in 1879 is believed to have been left by him.

There seems to be little doubt that the first European to sight Australia was Luis Vaez de Torres who saw Cape York at the northern tip of Queensland in July 1606. Later that year, the Dutch explorer Willem Janszoon sailed the *Duyfken* down the west coast of Cape

York. He did not realise that he was actually charting *Terra Australis*, believing that he was still exploring the coast of New Guinea.

In 1610, Henderik Brouwer crossed the Indian Ocean and successfully sailed up the coast of Western Australia. Six years later Dirk Hartog sailed too far and landed at Cape Inscription on 26 October 1616. It was here that Hartog left his famous pewter plate inscribed (in Dutch): '1616. On 25th October there arrived here the ship *Eendraght* of Amsterdam. Supercargo Gilles Miebais of Liege; skipper Dirck Hatichs of Amsterdam. On 27th do. she set sail again for Bantam. Subcargo Jan Stins; upper steersman Pieter Doores of Bil. In the year 1616.' By 1619, the Dutch had captured the main trading port on the island of Java, renamed it Batavia, and established it as the centre of Dutch influence in the East Indies. Seeking an easier route to the East Indies, Dutch sailors decided to sail across the Indian Ocean on the latitude of the Roaring Forties and then turn north. Inevitably

Above: The Dutch were great navigators and sailors whose exploration of the coast of Western Australia contributed to the European understanding of the continent. Here the Dutch vessel Mellish *enters Sydney Harbour in 1829.*

Above: Pirate and adventurer, William Dampier's dour late-17th century descriptions of Western Australia ensured that the British showed little interest in Australia for nearly a century.

Right: Dampier's A New Voyage Round the World *told of his dramatic adventures and was a best seller in England. Here, he and his crew battle a huge storm at sea.*

some ships sailed too far east and reached the coast of what is now Western Australia.

The Dutch exploration of the Australian coastline continued for most of the seventeenth century. Perhaps the most famous of all the explorers was Abel Tasman who, on two voyages in 1642 and 1644, discovered Van Diemen's Land (Tasmania) and explored large sections of the northern coastline of the continent. Tasman is credited with the discovery that Australia was not connected to Papua New Guinea and with giving the continent the name 'New Holland'.

The first Englishman to set foot on Australian soil was the pirate William Dampier who landed on the Western Australian coast in 1688 and 1699. His best-selling account of his first voyage, *A New Voyage Round the World*, had little to say in Australia's favour and probably dissuaded the British from further exploration of the country. He described the Aborigines as 'the miserablest people on earth' and reported that 'we Anchor'd at three several Places, and stay'd at the first of them (on the W. side of the Bay) till the 11th. During which time we searched about, as I said, for fresh Water, digging Wells, but to no purpose'. These were hardly descriptions to encourage further exploration or possible settlement.

CAPTAIN COOK'S ARRIVAL

While the Dutch were curious, they seemed to have little interest in settling Australia. It was not until the arrival of Captain James Cook that Europe was alerted to the full potential of the continent. In 1768, Cook, commanding HM Bark *Endeavour*, travelled to the South Seas to observe the transit of Venus and explore the 'Great South Land'. On 20 April 1770 Zachary Hicks, the First Lieutenant on the ship, sighted the coast of Australia.

It is one of the bitter ironies, and something which is hard to explain, that Cook saw Aborigines all the way up the coast and yet, on 22 August 1770, on Possession Island, he claimed all the eastern coast for King George III and named it New South Wales. It was, as history has shown, an extraordinary act. All the way up the coast, Cook saw the fires from Aboriginal camps and at numerous places he had sighted Aborigines on beaches and headlands and yet, in spite of British regulations regarding inhabited lands, he claimed the east coast as though it was uninhabited. Even the most cursory glance at Cook's journals reveals evidence of Aborigines, who were openly antagonistic to the arrival of these

Above: So much that is known about Australia's unique flora and fauna is the result of the work of Captain Cook's tireless botanist, Sir Joseph Banks.

Right: A romantic depiction of Governor Arthur Phillip watching as the Union Jack is raised at Farm Cove on the shores of Sydney Harbour on 26 January, 1788.

Europeans. The journal entry for 27 April 1770 recorded: 'The Indians who had not followed the boat, seeing the ship approach, used many threatening gestures and brandished their weapons; particularly two who made a very singular appearance, for their faces seemed to have been dusted with white powder and their bodies painted with broad streaks of the same colour which, passing obliquely over their breasts and backs, looked not unlike the cross-belts worn by our soldiers ... as we came in we saw, on both points of the bay, a few huts and several of the natives, men, women, and children.'

Nine years later, Sir Joseph Banks recommended Botany Bay as a suitable site for a penal colony to be established and in 1786 the British government authorised the sending of convicts to New South Wales.

EUROPEAN SETTLEMENT

The First Fleet brought approximately 1000 Europeans to Australia. The 11 ships of the fleet carried 759 convicts, 23 of whom died during the voyage and six children were born. After a journey of nine months, 1030 people landed, 736 of them convicts. Of the others there were 211 marines, 27 wives of officers, the Governor and his staff of nine.

The convicts that arrived at Port Jackson were transported simply because the gaols in Britain were overflowing. What followed was a period of approximately 50 years when a number of settlements in all states except South Australia were used to ease the pressure on British gaols. This was a period when the British were a great imperial power. The history of the colonies was characterised by exploration of the hinterland (always with assistance from Aborigines) and very rapid settlement of lands which were primarily used to produce goods which could be exported to Britain. This settlement was achieved by ruthless dispossession of the indigenous inhabitants with large-scale massacres being commonplace.

The colonisation process was never easy. In the early years there was a constant shortage of food and conflicts with Aborigines. The convicts were a constant source of violence and the land was harsh, quite unlike Britain, and prone to droughts, floods and bushfires.

Above: In the early years, the settlement at Port Jackson was little more than an isolated prison and a harbour as shown in this painting titled 'View from the Settlement on Sydney Cove, Port Jackson, 20th August 1788'.

Above: Australia's early history is full of men of great achievements. William Charles Wentworth was a politician, explorer, landowner, author and barrister.

EXPLORATION

From the moment the British arrived at Botany Bay and Sydney Cove they were eager to explore the vast unknown which lay beyond the shoreline. The first exploration impulse was driven by a mixture of necessity (the need to find fertile land so that the colony could become self-sufficient) and curiosity (the soldiers and convicts wanted to know what lay beyond the horizon). They dreamt of vast pasturelands which would make the new colony rich. Some convicts, understanding little of geography, believed they could walk from Sydney Town to Batavia (in Indonesia) and China. Some even believed that a white settlement existed beyond the mountains. There are numerous stories of convicts who escaped from Sydney and headed into the bush. They either died or 'went native', being accepted by the native Aborigines.

As early as March 1788 Governor Phillip and a small party reached the Pittwater area of Broken Bay to the north of Sydney and by April the northern shore of Sydney Harbour had been explored.

The most important of the early explorations was the crossing of the magnificent Blue Mountains west of Sydney. There was a widely held perception in the colony that the future of the continent would be determined by the richness of the land on the western side of these impenetrable canyons. Beginning in 1789, many hapless explorers tried various routes, until 1813 when Gregory Blaxland, William Charles Wentworth and William Lawson, who were watched all the way by Aborigines, finally succeeded. Two years later, a road across the mountains was built and in the next decade the European explorers pushed rapidly into the hinterland looking for good pastureland and grazing country. In 1817 and 1818, John Oxley pushed south and nearly reached the Murrumbidgee River and then headed north and reached the present site of Port Macquarie. In 1819, John Howe successfully travelled overland to the Hunter Valley, and in 1823 Captain Mark Currie explored the Lake George area near the present site of Canberra and pushed on until he reached the Murrumbidgee River.

In the 1820s and 1830s, the explorers reached into areas which would subsequently become parts of Queensland and South Australia. In 1824 Hamilton Hume and William Hovell explored from south of Sydney through to the Western Port district of Victoria. They had hoped to reach Port Phillip but they miscalculated. Three years later, in 1827, Allan Cunningham headed north from the Upper Hunter Valley and reached the Liverpool Plains and the rich Darling Downs. These expeditions were essentially pragmatic. In their wake came a series of dreamers who were more interested in mysteries, myths and achievements.

Charles Sturt was fascinated by the question: 'Why do so many of the rivers in New South Wales flow inland?' He wanted to discover whether or not Australia had a vast inland sea. Sturt's progress down the Murray River was assisted by a group of Aborigines. At one point the local community were so incensed by Sturt's appearance on their stretch of the river that they followed him threatening to wipe out the entire party. Sturt records: 'With every pacific disposition, and an extreme reluctance to take away life, I foresaw that it would be impossible any longer to avoid an engagement, yet with such fearful numbers against us I was doubtful of the result.' It was only when his guides arrived that he was saved from almost certain death. These events occurred at the point where the Murray and Darling rivers meet. In 1831, Major Thomas Mitchell explored the rivers in the north-west of New South Wales, and in 1835 he made an epic journey through western New South Wales and north-western Victoria where, after crossing numerous rivers, he came across rich pastoral land which he named 'Australia Felix'. All these journeys were characterised by bloody skirmishes with Aborigines. Perhaps the most infamous incident occurred on 26 May 1836 when Mitchell, at a place he later named Mount Dispersion, fired over 80 shots at a large

Above: Charles Sturt's 1830 exploration of the Murray and Darling rivers was facilitated by friendly Aborigines. At one point Sturt got ahead of his guides and he placed himself in great danger.

Above: Aborigines were unimpressed by the arrival of Europeans and frequently challenged their right to pass through or settle the land.

group of Aborigines. He later wrote: 'The Aborigines betook themselves to the river, my men pursuing them and shooting as many as they could. Numbers were shot swimming across the Murray, and some even after they had reached the opposite shore.' These conflicts between explorers and Aborigines were to become commonplace over the next 50 years. Such actions were always considered, as the history books record, to be a matter of the brave and adventurous explorers battling against wild and ignorant savages.

Throughout the 1850s, 1860s and 1870s many major explorations occurred. Robert O'Hara Burke, William Wills and John McDouall Stuart all crossed the continent from north to south, with assistance from Aborigines. Edward Eyre crossed the Great Australian Bight with the crucial assistance of an Aborigine named Wylie, and John Forrest, Alexander Forrest, Ernest Giles, Augustus Charles Gregory and Francis Thomas Gregory explored vast inland areas of Western Australia.

Above: Without the tireless assistance of his Aboriginal guide, Wylie, Edward Eyre would never have been able to cross the deserts which edge the Great Australian Bight.

Left: The race to be the first to cross the continent from north to south was financed by gold money from Victoria. It resulted in the deaths of the explorers Burke and Wills.

Slowly the continent was opened up. The dreams of vast pastures and of inland seas disappeared as explorer after explorer found that the inland reality was desert, heat, flies, disease and genuine hardship. Perhaps their greatest achievement was to discover that Australia has one of the largest desert areas on Earth.

By the end of the nineteenth century the European settlers had a substantial, if not comprehensive, understanding of the continent. They realised that clinging to the coast was a necessity because the inland was such a vast emptiness. Yet they did not realise that despite its problems, Aborigines had, through careful land management, settled the entire continent successfully. No matter where the explorers went—on the dry plains of the Nullarbor, in the dense tropical jungles of north Queensland, on the dry vastness of Queensland's Gulf country—there were always Aborigines. Over nearly 60 000 years these people had modified their lifestyle to suit the continent's diversity of climates.

Above: Between 1851 until 1954 (the year of the last gold mining in the district) a total of 25 million ounces of gold were taken from the area around Bendigo. Fossicking soon gave way to sophisticated operations like the Bendigo Garden Gully Claim.

DISCOVERY OF GOLD

The first discovery of gold had occurred as early as 1823 when J. McBrien, a government surveyor, found gold in the Fish River near Bathurst. Then in 1839 Paul Strzelecki found gold near Hartley. When news of the gold rush in California reached Australia there was an exodus of prospectors across the Pacific. This caused the New South Wales government, under Governor Fitzroy, to institute a policy of gold exploration in 1849.

The beginning of the Australian gold rushes occurred when Edward Hargraves, after 18 months of working on the Californian goldfields, returned to Australia believing that the area around Bathurst and Orange might contain gold. On 12 February 1851, at the junction of Summer Hill Creek and Lewis Ponds Creek, Hargraves and a colleague, John Lister, successfully panned gold. In April, Lister and two brothers, James and William Tom, found gold at Ophir. In May 1851, Hargraves took 120 grams of gold to Sydney and showed it to

the Colonial Secretary, and on 14 May the gold discovery was announced. Within days men were pouring into the Ophir area. The gold rush had started.

Only six weeks after the Ophir announcement, James Esmond found substantial gold deposits near Clunes, and over the next eight months, the vast deposits at Ballarat and Bendigo had been discovered. Although the majority of gold rushes occurred in the 1850s, prospectors continued to find new goldfields, particularly in Western Australia and Queensland, from the 1860s to the 1890s. In Queensland there were a series of gold rushes in the 1870s to places which appeared and disappeared as the miners rushed to the diggings and then rushed on to the next goldfield. In Western Australia gold discovery only occurred in the 1880s and 1890s, with lodes being found in the Kimberley and Pilbara regions and major finds in the Kalgoorlie and Coolgardie fields.

The last region of Australia to be mined was the Northern Territory where successful gold discovery peaked in 1894 when over one million grams were discovered.

Above: Overnight the Australian bush was turned into bustling towns by gold fever. At its height the New South Wales town of Gulgong had a population of 20 000 people all seeking their fortune.

Above: Throughout the 19th century people from all over Britain poured into Australia. These Scottish immigrants risked everything hoping for a new and better life.

EMERGENCE OF MULTICULTURALISM

Australia's multicultural society has grown as a result of internal and external factors. Some groups of people were transported as convicts, some fled from their homelands to seek refuge from war, some were invited by the government to begin a new work life, and some came to find riches in the discovery of gold.

The diversity of the first group of settlers and convicts provided a tentative beginning to what would become a multicultural society. Perhaps the most significant group of convicts were the Irish Catholics. They constantly challenged the nation's perception of itself as Anglo-Saxon, Protestant and elitist. By 1853, when transportation to eastern Australia ended, a total of 29 466 Irish men and 9104 Irish women, nearly one-quarter of all convicts, had arrived in Australia. From the earliest times the country was always looking for labour. It was this that led to the emigration of nearly 500 labourers from the Indian subcontinent between 1837–44, and from 1838–39 a group of some 500 Lutherans from

Klemzig in Prussian Silesia arrived in South Australia. Both groups were typical of the country's very slow movement towards multiculturalism.

A small group present among the first convicts were the Jews. No-one knows the precise number but there were between eight and 14 Jewish convicts on the First Fleet. In 1851, there were 2000 Jews in Australia. A decade later, largely due to the gold rushes which brought people from all over the world, the Jewish population had grown to 5000. In the 1880s, a wave of anti-Semitism in Eastern Europe saw tens of thousands of Jews fleeing from Russia and Poland. In the twentieth century the rise of Nazism brought another wave of immigration—by 1938, 2000 Jews from Germany, Austria and the former Czechoslovakia were seeking refugee status in Australia every week.

By far the most significant non-European emigration to Australia started between 1848 and 1852 when 3000 Chinese arrived to work as indentured labourers on farms. In

Above: Ships from throughout the world brought migrants to Australia. Inevitably most of the migrants settled in the port cities. Today nearly 90 per cent of Australians live in urban areas.

Above: Europeans went to the goldfields as individuals, however, the Chinese worked in teams. By 1858 there were more than 40 000 Chinese on the Victorian goldfields.

Victoria in 1854 there were only 2000 Chinese; but by 1858 there were an estimated 40 000 as a result of the gold rushes. By 1861, 60 per cent of all the people on the New South Wales goldfields and 25 per cent of the people on the Victorian goldfields were Chinese. This massive influx of Chinese workers challenged the essentially European nature of Australian society. There were race riots on the goldfields and by 1855 Victoria had enacted legislation to restrict the entry of Chinese to the colony. This was followed by restrictive legislation in South Australia (1857) and New South Wales (1861), later repealed by the end of the decade. They were the precursors to Australia's infamous 'White Australia' policy, a widely used term to describe all government legislation which favoured Europeans and seemed to discriminate against Asians and other non-white racial groups. A second wave of Chinese immigration occurred in the 1880s when gold was discovered in the Northern Territory and northern Queensland.

From 1863–1904, 61 160 Pacific Islanders arrived to work on the Queensland canefields. These immigrants, known as 'kanakas', were indentured labourers who worked in a state of virtual slavery. The first kanakas arrived from the New Hebrides and Loyalty Islands aboard the 100-tonne schooner, *Don Juan*, on 15 August 1863. This form of unambiguous slavery was eventually stopped in 1904. Today there are substantial numbers of descendants of kanakas still living in Queensland.

After World War II, frightened by the perception that the country was in imminent danger from its northern neighbours (a fear which had been exacerbated by the Japanese invasion of Indonesia, Papua New Guinea and northern Australia), Australia began an active campaign to attract migrants of European descent. British migrants were offered assisted passages from 1947 until 1972, when the program was expanded to other countries. By the mid-1970s, Australia had immigration assistance plans in place with Italy, Greece, Holland, West Germany, Yugoslavia, Poland and Austria.

This post-war immigration boom brought one million migrants to Australia by 1955. The first wave brought refugees from war-torn Europe, mainly from Eastern Europe. The second wave in the 1950s and early 1960s came from Mediterranean countries. The 1960s were a period of great prosperity and most Australian manufacturers could not have functioned without migrant labour.

Although Italian immigration to Australia was essentially a post-war phenomenon, there was one convict of Italian descent on the First Fleet. By 1933 the number had grown to 26 500. Already the Italians had become Australia's largest immigrant group after the British and the Irish, resulting in racial tensions. In spite of this discord, an agreement was reached between Australia and Italy after World War II for the Australian government to provide

assisted passage to selected Italian families. From 1945–1973, 379 000 Italians immigrated to Australia. Most of the important post-war industrial development of Australia involved Italian workers. Italians saw Australia as a land of opportunity and, in substantial numbers, they gradually left labouring to establish their own businesses. By the 1980s, more than 20 per cent of first-generation Italians were self-employed, operating grocery and fruit stores, cafés and restaurants, and running their own construction companies.

The fourth-largest ethnic group in Australia are the Greeks. After the British, Irish and Italians they form a significant minority, with over half a million Australians claiming Greek ancestry. Few Greeks came to Australia at the time of the gold rushes. In fact, as late as 1891 there were less than 500 Greeks living in Australia, and by 1939 this number had only risen to 15 000. The major period of Greek immigration started with a government program of assisted passage in the early 1950s. From 1953–56 over 30 000 Greeks arrived in Australia. This pattern of migration continued into the 1960s with an average of nearly 16 000 Greeks arriving to settle in Australia each year.

By 1991 there were 75 400 Lebanese living in Australia. They had been arriving since the 1950s but, with the beginning of an extended period of civil unrest and religious

Above: By the end of World War II Australia was still underpopulated and active programs of immigration, almost exclusively from Europe, were undertaken.

Above: More than one million migrants arrived in Australia between 1945–55. Of that number one-third came from Italy. To Australia's great benefit they brought both their culture and their food.

conflict in their homeland during the 1970s, the trickle soon became a flood with many people applying for entry under refugee status.

Australia resisted settlement by Asians and actively discouraged Asian immigration for about 100 years after the nineteenth-century gold rushes, in spite of its geographic position among Asian neighbours. This changed slowly. In the 1950s, the Colombo Plan brought students to Australia from various Asian countries—notably Singapore, Malaysia, Pakistan, India and later Vietnam, Thailand and Cambodia. Their numbers increased as Australia permitted fee-paying students from Asia to study at secondary and tertiary educational institutions. In 1956 Asians who had lived in Australia for more than 15 years could become naturalised Australians. Two years later, the 1901 *Immigration Restriction Act* (legislation designed to prohibit the permanent settlement in Australia of non-Europeans) was abolished, and by the 1970s, a steady trickle of people from Japan and South-East Asia were coming to Australia.

Asians are continuing to settle in Australia in increasing numbers. In 1991 the number of Australians of South-East Asian origin was 404 600. The increase of immigrants from North-East Asia was even greater, with the largest Asian groups in Australia in 1991 being from Vietnam (133 400), Malaysia (84 100), Philippines (74 300), Hong Kong (73 200), China (68 500) and India (65 400).

Australia today is a genuinely multicultural society. Over the past two centuries, various migrant groups have produced a society which, while English speaking and still committed to many British legal and political structures, holds a diverse mixture of races, cultures, religions and customs.

However, whether or not Australia is a successful multicultural society is almost impossible to measure. Modern Australian society is in a state of flux. Its immigration policies, particularly since the 1950s, have been dramatic and have created far-reaching implications for the way Australians view themselves.

Above: So many immigrants had their first experience of urban Australia when, having passed through Sydney Heads, they gazed on the distinctive 'coathanger' shape of the Sydney Harbour Bridge.

Above: In spite of growing multiculturalism Australia still showed allegiance to Britain. It was all pomp and ceremony for a visit from the Duke and Duchess of York.

FEDERATION

Since European settlement, the geopolitical boundaries of Australia's states and colonies have changed many times throughout the continent.

In 1825 Van Diemen's Land was constituted as a separate colony and was renamed Tasmania in 1855. South Australia was created on 15 August 1834 by King William IV. In 1851, the colony of Victoria, previously known as the Port Phillip District, was constituted. The last state to emerge was Queensland, which was finally granted an independent administration on 6 June 1859. The Australian Capital Territory, carved out of New South Wales, was handed over to the new federal government in 1911. The Northern Territory was moved from South Australia to the Commonwealth in 1911, carved up into North and Central Australia between 1926 and 1931, and eventually granted its own elected administration in 1976.

It was always impractical that these separate colonies could exist independently of one another and therefore there was an inevitable movement towards Federation. In the 1850s there was a London-based General Association for the Australian Colonies but, with interstate rivalries and a lack of any feeling of national identity, it was never anything more than an interesting idea. During the 1860s and 1870s the colonies moved further apart as some colonies prospered and others declined. This resulted in different levels of taxation, problems with interstate taxes and separate policies on immigration, tariffs and defence. The problems became so great that, during the course of the 1880 intercolonial conference, Henry Parkes, an Australian politician at the time, recommended the establishment of a permanent Federal Council. It was only supported by South Australia, Tasmania and New South Wales, and seemed destined to fail. However, it was around this time that Germany and France began showing interest in colonising the Pacific, and the fear of war and possible conflict pushed those states which had baulked at a Federal Council to recognise its value. On 24 October 1889 at Tenterfield in northern New South Wales, Parkes addressed a meeting and argued persuasively that Australia had to develop a national defence force. Historians consider this speech to be the true starting point for the movement which culminated in Federation 11 years later.

Over the next decade, debate raged but there was a mood of change in the air and it was now impossible for any of the state governments to resist. Thus, on 22 March 1897, after enabling legislation had been passed in every state apart from Queensland, a Federal Convention was held in Adelaide. Two further sessions were held in Sydney and Melbourne in September 1897 and January 1898 respectively. By 13 March 1898 a draft constitution had been completed and in early June that same year the voters of New South Wales, Victoria, Tasmania and South Australia went to the polls. The result was 219 712 for Federation and 108 363 against, with Victoria recording an extraordinary 100 520 for and only 22 099 against.

The final process required the bill to be taken to London to be enacted into legislation by the British Parliament. On 17 September 1900 Queen Victoria signed a proclamation approving the establishment of the Federation on the first day of the new century and thus, on 1 January 1901 the Commonwealth of Australia became a reality.

Above: Known as the father of Australian Federation, Henry Parkes was a tireless advocate of a federal government although tragically he died before Federation occurred.

Above: The height of modernity and sophistication. Trams make their way up Flinders Street in Melbourne, in the early years of this century.

MODERN AUSTRALIA

Australia in the twentieth century has grown to be a confident nation actively involved in the development and prosperity of its own region and trying to establish itself in the broader international community.

It has been a painful and often complex journey involving the search for a national identity, an inordinate pride in physical attributes (both in war and on the sporting field),

Above: Australia was finally linked to the rest of the world when this first telegram arrived from England. Suddenly we didn't feel quite so isolated anymore.

Left: Surf lifesaving officially started in 1907 as more and more Australians headed for the beach during the summer. The lifesaver was to become a potent symbol of the new country.

the need to break from the narrow cultural values established by a predominantly Anglo-Saxon society, and the need to acknowledge the true history of the country.

As many European visitors note with some amusement, we are also a nation which likes to be told how to behave. We seem to like the idea of government agencies telling us to cover ourselves with protective lotions before we go out in the sun. We enjoy being constantly reminded that we are killing each other on the roads (road toll figures are a regular feature of national news bulletins). We are proud of the surf lifesaving movement, which sees public-minded people protecting foolish people who swim where they shouldn't. And we have even had a major national program to encourage us all to keep fit.

The search for some kind of national identity started almost immediately after Federation. It was always going to be a challenge because Europeans had not had enough time to establish themselves on the land. As a nation we came into existence only after the invention of the motor car and electricity, which are prevailing means of transport and communication, so we are a truly modern society where distinct regional styles of housing, languages and accents did not have time to develop.

The first defining event in the nation's history was World War I where, still tied by complex obligations to Britain, Australia sent vast numbers of young soldiers to European

Above: Australia's great defining moment as a nation occurred in 1914 when young ANZAC soldiers landed at Gallipoli on the coast of Turkey.

battlefields. About 59 330 Australians died on foreign soil thousands of miles from their homeland. In spite of its distance from Australian shores, and the sense that Australian troops were fighting the war of others, it is within the larger context of the war, and particularly the near-massacre of Australian troops at Gallipoli, that the first myth of the 'Australian character' was wrought. The image of the Australian soldier was one of a bronzed Anzac, fiercely independent, a natural sportsman, eager for fair play, deeply committed to his 'mates' and worshipping the idea that he lived in the greatest country on Earth where individual enterprise triumphed.

In the late twentieth century, we are more realistic about our image. We are an urban community (over 80 per cent of Australians live in large towns and cities), basically indistinct from many other parts of the world. We watch American and British movies and television, shop in large modern shopping malls, drive cars manufactured all over the world, listen to the same pop music as the rest of the English-speaking world, read the same international bestsellers and so on.

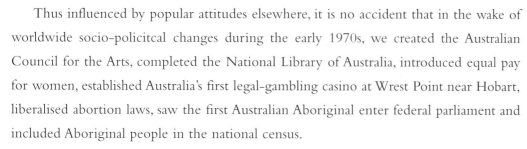

Above: One war which was not greeted with universal approval was the 1960s war in Vietnam which led to massive street protests throughout the country.

Left: Many times this century Australian soldiers have fought in wars overseas. Their return and departure have always been moments of great emotion for the entire nation.

Thus influenced by popular attitudes elsewhere, it is no accident that in the wake of worldwide socio-policitcal changes during the early 1970s, we created the Australian Council for the Arts, completed the National Library of Australia, introduced equal pay for women, established Australia's first legal-gambling casino at Wrest Point near Hobart, liberalised abortion laws, saw the first Australian Aboriginal enter federal parliament and included Aboriginal people in the national census.

The fight for land rights, which was to dominate Aboriginal thinking throughout the 1970s and 1980s, experienced both victories and defeats. In January 1971, the Victorian government announced that the Aboriginal reserves at Lake Tyers in the Gippsland region and around Framlington would be handed over to the local Aboriginal communities. However, in April the people of Yirrkala lost their land rights battle in the Northern Territory Supreme Court. The decision to grant leasehold title to the Gurundji people in 1975 was the beginning of a process which culminated in the admission that land had been taken from Aborigines. The historic *Mabo* decision of 1992 attempted to

Above: It may be mythic but it is also true. Australian culture is about sun, sand and surf. We cling to the coast of the continent and we love the lifestyle afforded by summer at the beach.

further redress the land issue by refuting the long-held claim that the land was uninhabited when the Europeans arrived, opening up the opportunity for many more land claims to reach the courts.

True reconciliation, in spite of the protestations of politicians, could still be years away. The High Court's *Wik* decision in 1998 established that pastoral leases could not extinguish Native Title. In 1998 the Liberal-National Party government's '10 Point Plan' was passed into law and sustains the on-going issue of Aboriginal land rights.

So who is the modern Australian? Throughout the century, images of Australia have ranged from bronzed Anzacs to urbane city dwellers. The enduring images have always contained elements of sturdy independence, a refusal to respect authority, a genuine sense of egalitarianism, a dislike of pretentiousness and a sense of energy and exuberance. Whether Australians live in cities (as most people do) or work in the 'outback', these qualities endure.

Above: Rejoicing in our eccentricity. The Todd River Boat Race on the dry riverbed of the Todd River in Alice Springs.

Far left: The largest celebration of Gay Pride in the world, Sydney's Mardi Gras attracts over 500 000 people each year.

Left: Multiculturalism in all its glory. A dancer from a folkloric group at the Adelaide Arts Festival.

NEW SOUTH WALES

THE PREMIER STATE

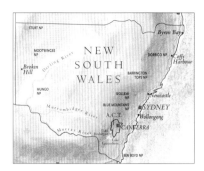

THE PREMIER STATE

With nearly six million residents, New South Wales accounts for more than a third of the nation's population and Sydney with its world-famous Opera House and Harbour Bridge is usually the first destination for most tourists. From its origins as a penal settlement, the success of New South Wales today is based upon the strength and diversity of its economic base, the richness of its cultural mix and its outstanding natural and man-made icons. New South Wales is hosting the Year 2000 Olympic Games in Sydney, and the wilderness areas in the Blue Mountains are undergoing approval for World Heritage listing. Such diverse events demonstrate the outstanding potential and capability of this state, with its ever-changing landscape and strong historical presence.

EUROPEAN SETTLEMENT

The genesis of New South Wales occurred on Possession Island at the tip of Cape York on 22 August 1770 when Captain James Cook claimed more than half of the continent of Australia in the name of King George III, the reigning British monarch, pre-empting the establishment of a penal colony 15 years later at Port Jackson. Cook did not name the east coast as soon as he claimed it—the term 'New South Wales' came to him on the homeward journey and he recorded it in his journal.

The decision to create a penal colony in New South Wales was the result of the American War of Independence, which eliminated North America as a suitable penal colony, as well as the overcrowding in British prisons caused by a rise in crime at the time of the Industrial Revolution.

Above: The country's European founding father, Captain Arthur Phillip, a Londoner from a modest background, administered the convict colony of Sydney Town from 1788-1792.

Opposite: The beginning of the European story of Australia. The ships of the First Fleet moored in Sydney Harbour in January, 1788.

Previous pages: The incessant waves of the Pacific Ocean break all along the east coast of New South Wales.

Above: A vital and illuminating source of information about the early colony. Captain Phillip's 'Narrative' of the First Fleet published in London in 1789.

In his speech to the British Parliament in January 1787, King George III referred to the proposal to send an expedition to Botany Bay as another attempt to 'remove the inconvenience which arose from the crowded state of the gaols in different parts of the Kingdom'. And so on 13 May 1787 the First Fleet set sail from Portsmouth. It consisted of eleven ships: two escorts, HMS *Sirius* and HMS *Supply*; six transport ships; and three store ships. After a journey of nine months, 1030 people landed, 736 of them convicts.

On 18 January 1788 Governor Phillip reached Botany Bay on HMS *Supply*. Their first encounter with local Aborigines was not friendly. Phillip recorded: 'We went a little way up the bay to look for water, but finding none we returned abreast of the *Supply*, where we observed a group of natives. We put the boats on shore near where we observed two of their canoes lying. They immediately got up and called to us in a menacing tone, and at the same time brandishing their spears or lances.' Recalling this first contact many years later an Aborigine named Mahroot, a member of the Botany Bay tribe, noted: 'They thought they was the devil when they landed first, they did not know what to make of them. When they saw them going up the masts they thought they was opossums.'

Phillip was not impressed by Botany Bay. The lack of fresh water made the site unsuitable so he proceeded immediately to Port Jackson, a short distance to the north. It was, in Phillip's famous expression, 'the finest harbour in the world' and so, within a week the entire fleet had moved north and the colony of Sydney had begun. On 26 January the British flag was raised at Sydney Cove and Phillip told the convicts that he hoped the new colony would bring them 'reformation, happiness, and prosperity'.

However, the early colony was fraught with problems, the biggest one being food because both Sydney Cove and the new arrivals were unsuited for agriculture. There were few tools and the average convict (30 per cent were Londoners) had no agricultural skills. Phillip therefore established a series of settlements in the hope that some of them would become agriculturally productive.

By July 1788 the colony's food problems were becoming critical. Governor Phillip wrote to the British Under-Secretary of State stating that food supplies were so low that male convicts 'Each received 7 pounds of bread or in lieu thereof 7 pounds of flour, 7 pounds of beef or in lieu thereof pork, 3 pints of pease, 6 ounces of butter', and female convicts were receiving two-thirds of those rations. By September 1788 the situation was so bad that the last cow had been killed for meat and the HMS *Sirius* had been despatched to Cape Town to bring back any food it could get. It returned in May 1789 with 6.5 tonnes of flour having circumnavigated the world in the Roaring Forties. However, in November 1789 supplies were still so low that everyone had their already limited rations reduced to

two-thirds. By April only six weeks of rations remained. Rations were reduced even more and the whole colony focused on catching fish in the harbour and trying to trap kangaroos and wallabies in the hinterland. Convicts who stole food were being sentenced to 2000 lashes. On 3 June the Second Fleet sailed into the harbour with a number of store ships carrying adequate supplies to save the colony. With the Second Fleet came instructions to settle the land as quickly as possible and to produce food by any possible means.

By 1791 land had been granted to over 150 people in the hope that the agricultural base of the infant settlement could be broadened. However, there was still a lack of expertise and Phillip eventually pleaded with the British government to send out free settlers with farming experience so that New South Wales could become self-sufficient. This call was answered, and by the mid-1790s, farms, with convicts as labourers, were providing Sydney with supplies. Within four years Phillip had found water, settled the land and made it productive, converting Sydney into a viable colony and setting the base upon which New South Wales was created.

Above: While Sydney Cove may have offered only a hard life for the convicts, life for the Governor was similar to that in England. By 1791, the Governor's residence had been built and offered this fine view across the harbour. The new colony was slowly growing around the shoreline.

Above: To the west of Sydney lie the box canyons of the Blue Mountains. It wasn't until 1813 that Europeans first gazed out on the famous Three Sisters from the cliffs at Katoomba.

EXPLORATION OF THE STATE

It was during this time that the exploration of New South Wales by Europeans started in earnest. The eastern half of the continent was considered part of New South Wales so that the exploration of the coast, from the discovery of the Hunter River to the circumnavigation of Van Diemen's Land, was seen as part of the larger exploration of this state.

The great challenge, however, lay inland from Sydney. The Blue Mountains to the west seemed impassable to many European explorers, who made their way across the Sydney basin only to be hindered by the towering escarpments and wild river countryside of the Grose and Kanangra regions (now National Parks). When the mountains were finally crossed in 1813 by the explorers Blaxland, Wentworth and Lawson, it was merely a question of time before the whole of New South Wales was settled, opening up the rich pasturelands which lay beyond the mountains.

It is appropriate that this exploration was achieved during the governorship of Lachlan Macquarie, Governor from 1810 to 1823, who transformed the struggling colony into a thriving and successful region. During his administration, numerous public buildings were constructed with the help of the gifted ex-convict Francis Greenway; education and the treatment of women and children were improved; the first bank (the Bank of New South Wales) was granted a charter; and exploration and settlement proceeded at a dramatic pace. By the time Macquarie returned to England, the colony had been explored from Port Macquarie in the north to the Lachlan and Macquarie rivers in the west and Jervis Bay in the south. Once the Blue Mountains had been crossed, explorers headed off in every direction—Hamilton Hume and William Hovell journeyed from Sydney to the present-day site of Melbourne, Charles Sturt explored the inland rivers, Allan Cunningham and others found an inland route from Sydney to the present-day site of Brisbane, and Thomas Mitchell reached far into the outback of the state.

As the explorers opened up the country, they were followed by settlers. These were tough men (rarely accompanied by women and children) who with the assistance of labourers (often convicts) took herds of sheep and cattle to the limits of European settlement and simply 'squatted' on land. They were in constant conflict with Aborigines and, because they were beyond the law, they settled their disputes themselves. A small number befriended the Aborigines, reaching a peaceful understanding. The majority, however, ran the Aborigines off the land by dispersing or shooting and indiscriminately killing them.

DISCOVERY OF GOLD

While this unhappy chapter in Australia's history was occurring, New South Wales (still over half of the continent) was starting to be rather dramatically trimmed. In 1825 Van Diemen's Land was separated, followed in 1851 by Victoria and 1859 by Queensland, each being given some measure of autonomy.

New South Wales' focus on agriculture during this period resulted in a population of 2.75 million sheep by 1838. It appeared that the colony's future was going to be essentially rural, when the history of both New South Wales and the rest of Australia was miraculously transformed in 1851 by the discovery of gold at Ophir near Bathurst.

Gold fever saw the virtual collapse of agriculture as poorly paid farm workers downed tools and headed for the goldfields. Under such circumstances it was impossible for large numbers of convicts to continue to be incarcerated (convict labour often constituted working on the farms of free settlers) and rapidly transportation from England came to an end. Miners and prospectors from all over the world flocked to Sydney, eager to get to the goldfields.

With the gold rush came a form of independence. The British handed over control of land policy to the New South Wales Legislative Council in 1852 and a form of responsible government was granted when, in 1855, the Legislative Assembly, was created.

Above: Beyond the Great Dividing Range were vast pasturelands where the new explorers grazed sheep and cattle much to the annoyance of the local Aborigines.

Above: A triumph of civil construction, the Sydney Harbour Bridge. When it was built in 1932 it was the largest steel arch bridge in the world. It carried traffic 132 metres above sea level and, in its construction, 52 800 tonnes of steel had been used.

DEVELOPMENT OF THE PREMIER STATE

In the decade from 1851 to 1861 the population of the state nearly doubled from 197 000 to 350 000. The wealthy rural landowners who had traditionally controlled the state were now in a minority as the state became increasingly urbanised and as the cities of Sydney, Newcastle and Wollongong began to dominate the state's economy.

The state continued to develop throughout the 1870s and 1880s. Railways were built across the Blue Mountains and the combination of railway lines and Cobb & Co. coaches and bullock wagons (which had to travel on appalling bush tracks) opened up the state. The returned prosperity of the agricultural sector of the state's economy in the last years of the nineteenth century ensured an enduring and strong economic base.

The period leading up to the outbreak of World War I was a boom time for New South Wales. The area of the state growing wheat, greatly helped by the Federation strain of the grain developed by William Farrer, expanded to a massive 1.4 million hectares. The advent of refrigeration meant that meat could be safely exported to overseas markets. Discoveries of coal and other industrial metals saw the creation of industrial cities at Broken Hill, Newcastle and Port Kembla. At the time the state government was fiercely protectionist and this ensured that local industries, protected from overseas competition, grew rapidly.

The outbreak of World War I fuelled this already buoyant economy and by 1918 New South Wales had the strongest economic base in Australia. It has never really retreated from this position of economic dominance.

The period between the wars was a time of prosperity. Large numbers of Europeans—mainly from Great Britain although there were numbers fleeing from central Europe by the late 1930s—added to the state's growing population. Sydney grew dramatically. It was during this time that the Sydney Harbour Bridge was built and the city got its first underground rail network. Inevitably the Depression had a profound impact on the state's economy, but World War II saw many of the unemployed heading off to war and the economy, particularly that of the industrial cities of Newcastle and Wollongong, was kick-started by wartime requirements.

Above: The discovery of coal at Mount Kembla south of Sydney led to the development of a tiny port at Wollongong. Today it is no more than an old lighthouse and mooring for a small fishing fleet.

After the War, New South Wales enjoyed unrivalled prosperity. New railway lines criss-crossed the state and provided the vital infrastructure to allow farmers to get their produce easily to the coast. Large capital works saw full employment. In an era where life was relatively uncomplicated, local tragedies and triumphs took on a special meaning. The floods in Maitland in 1955 saw the entire town covered in water, and when 11 were killed, the disaster prompted statewide public sympathy.

The arrival of the young Queen Elizabeth and her new husband Prince Philip in 1954 was a reminder of the state's deep commitment to Britain. Wherever the Queen went, tens of thousands of flag-waving patriots gathered to demonstrate their allegiance. The popularity of the monarchy being more alive than ever.

SNOWY MOUNTAINS SCHEME

After World War II, the state embarked on the huge Snowy Mountains Hydro-Electricity scheme. By any measure it was a miracle of engineering. The logic of the project was inescapable. Each spring, melted snow waters flooded the rivers and drained the mountain range to the east, while to the west vast lands had to rely on unreliable rainfall and streams that ran dry. If the waters of the Snowy Mountains could be dammed and diverted, western New South Wales and Victoria could become reliably productive and, as a by-product, the waters could provide vast quantities of electricity to these two most populous states. The idea was hardly a new one. As early as the 1880s there had been suggestions of diverting the rivers but they had always be touted in seasons of drought and forgotten about when the weather improved. In 1908 New South Wales granted the Commonwealth government rights to the waters of the Snowy Mountains as a source of hydro-electric power.

In 1949 the project started and it was effectively completed when Tumut 3 Power Station began operation in 1973. During that time, over 100 000 people of 30 nationalities, working from 10 major towns and over 100 camps, built 1600 kilometres of roads, 16 large dams, 80 kilometres of aqueducts and over 140 kilometres of tunnels. The result was a hydro-electric scheme with a generating capacity of 3 740 000 kilowatts which could divert 2 350 000 millilitres of water for irrigation.

The benefits to many areas were enormous. The roads to the ski fields would never have been constructed without the Snowy Mountains Authority. Access to Australia's high country became available to everyone. This whole area is now one of Australia's premier holiday destinations, attracting skiiers during the winter months and walkers during the summer months when the alpine meadows are covered with wild flowers.

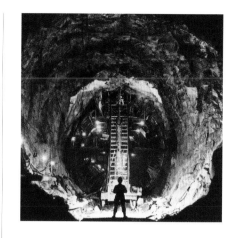

Above: The Snowy Mountains Hydro-Electricity Scheme in the 1950s provided the state with vast electricity reserves and diverted the waters from the melting snow to the parched inland of the state.

Opposite: A wilderness area of exceptional beauty, and the state's most popular skiing destination, the Kosciuszko National Park.

Following pages: Dense undergrowth and endless gum trees reaching for the sun in the Burrawang State Forest.

Above: The combination of warm subtropical temperatures and reliable rainfall attracted dairy and cattle farmers to the rich pasturelands of the Bellingen Valley in northern New South Wales.

FABRIC OF THE STATE

New South Wales is a thriving and complex state. It is now truly multicultural, boasting remarkable situations as the rural township of Griffith where 65 per cent of the community can trace their ancestry back to Italy; the city of Wollongong where the Nan Tien Temple is the largest Buddhist temple in the southern hemisphere; and the Sydney suburb of Granville where the local Iman calls the Muslim faithful to prayer.

As the state with the largest population, New South Wales can attract business, although current globalisation trends mean that Sydney continues to grow while rural areas, particularly those beyond the Great Dividing Range, have struggled to compete in world markets where the prices of wool, wheat, beef and fruit products have been falling. The rationalisation of industries has also seen many basic services—particularly banks and hospitals—disappearing from smaller rural communities. However, the awarding of the 2000 Olympics has seen massive building projects occur in Sydney accompanied by a spirit of optimism and prosperity.

Above: Positioned at the mouth of the Nambucca River, Nambucca Heads is a popular tourist destination on the New South Wales north coast with a careful combination of holiday attractions and peacefulness.

Above: To the locals, and to many visitors, Sydney Harbour is simply the most beautiful harbour in the world with the gentle sails of the Opera House setting off the gracious arc of the bridge.

GROWTH OF SYDNEY

Until the 1950s, Sydney, the capital of New South Wales was, by world standards, relatively small both in size and population. It had grown as a series of suburban layers around the central business district which, in turn, had evolved from the convict settlement at Port Jackson. At this time, the central business district was the centre of the city. To the west, the city effectively stopped at Parramatta, 23 kilometres from the city centre. Beyond it lay a number of semi-rural and isolated town-suburbs—St Marys, Emu Plains, Liverpool,

Campbelltown, Camden and Blacktown—which had small pockets of industry or were part of the city's market gardens.

In the space of less than 40 years, this entire area saw unprecedented growth. Symbolic of this change is the fact that between 1950 and 1990 the 'centre' of Sydney moved west to Parramatta. The greater west is now the economic powerhouse of the city and is therefore effectively the economic powerhouse of the entire country. It now covers an area of 8000 square hectares and generates an annual gross domestic product of $A34 billion, more than 20 per cent of the entire state of New South Wales' output and production.

Above: Sydneysiders love a party. New Years Eve, Boxing Day, Australia Day and Mardi Gras all attract hundreds of thousands of people to the city centre.

Above: A new and spectacular addition to the city is Stadium Australia, the main venue for the 2000 Olympics.

Right: Sydney Tower at Centrepoint is surrounded by the high rise office blocks which characterise Sydney's central business district.

While this development occurred, the centre of the city was also changing. The internationally famous Opera House, opened in 1973, gave Sydney a new air of sophistication, and the large influxes of migrants gave the state a decidedly multicultural ambience.

Perhaps a symbol of the state's sense of optimism and its belief that it will grow and prosper occurred when, on 23 September 1993, it was awarded the 2000 Olympics. This victory saw a massive series of building projects occur in Sydney, which eagerly awaits the arrival of 10200 athletes and the prospect of showing itself as a most beautiful city to an anticipated 3.5 billion people around the world.

VICTORIA

THE GARDEN STATE

THE GARDEN STATE

Victoria enjoys a unique position in Australian history. Until 1851 it was part of New South Wales then, in a period of 40 years, it became the premier state due to the vast wealth being generated by its goldfields. This wealth turned Melbourne into the financial and administrative centre of Australia, a position the city enjoyed at the time of Federation and still, to some extent, enjoys today. Certainly Melbourne was the de facto capital of the new country until the formal opening of Parliament House in Canberra in 1927—until the 1960s, many of the Commonwealth government's head offices were located in Melbourne.

The state has a rich architectural heritage, ranging from colonial miners' cottages to stately buildings in Melbourne, reflecting its history as a point of finance, learning, sport and art. Victoria's stunning coastline, climaxing with the Twelve Apostles, makes visiting the state a memorable experience.

In many ways Victoria is an incongruity which clashes with Australian stereotypes. It calls itself 'The Garden State' in a country famous for its desert landscapes. Its towns and landscapes are characterised by intimacy where much of the rest of the country is famous for its vast, open landscapes. It is a conservative state in a tough, working-class culture. It is these differences which sets Victoria apart from other mainland states.

EUROPEAN SETTLEMENT AND EXPLORATION

It has been estimated that in 1788, when the First Fleet sailed up the coast of Victoria towards Botany Bay, there were probably about 11 500 Aborigines living in Victoria, with most living along the coastline in small groups of 20 to 60 people.

Above: Determined to stop French settlement of Australia, Lieutenant David Collins landed on the shores of Port Phillip. This was to become the city of Melbourne.

Opposite: By 1851 Melbourne had grown from a small colonial outpost to be the capital of a new state. In a few years the discovery of gold would make it Australia's richest city.

Previous pages: Cape Woolamai Fauna Reserve, Phillip Island.

Above: The ruthlessly entrepreneurial John Batman who 'bought' Melbourne from the local Aborigines for some blankets, knives and provisions.

The European settlement of Victoria, like so much of Australia, was a result of the fear of possible French settlement. Lieutenant David Collins, accompanied by a party comprising both convicts and free settlers, landed on the shores of Port Phillip (near the modern day site of Sorrento) in October 1803 and a short-lived colony was established which immediately met with resistance from Aborigines. By May 1804 Collins had permission to move the colony to Van Diemen's Land.

It wasn't until the 1820s that pressure began to be exerted for a permanent settlement in Victoria. European explorers headed south from Sydney looking for good land. Hamilton Hume and William Hovell reached Port Phillip in 1824. They mistook it for Western Port and two years later, acting on their incorrect advice, a military and convict outpost was established there. It lasted 13 months.

In 1830 Charles Sturt explored the northern reaches of the state when he travelled along the Murray and Murrumbidgee rivers. Around this time John Batman, who was living in Van Diemen's Land, tried to gain approval from the Governor of New South Wales to settle the area around Western Port. He had been encouraged by reports that the land was fertile and the pastures were rich. The Governor, fearing problems if a second colony was created, denied Batman permission. In early 1835, however, Batman crossed Bass Strait and on 6 June 1835, in an extraordinary deal with no basis in law, infamously 'purchased' the land on the western shore of Port Phillip from the local Aborigines for the price of some blankets, knives and provisions. Batman soon chose a site for a village, and within a year the township of Melbourne began to grow on the banks of the Yarra River.

The subsequent exploration of Victoria occurred rapidly, and by 1845, squatters had occupied nearly all of the Western District, settled along the Murray River and moved down into the Gippsland area.

Most of these settlements took place with considerable violence and, realising the depth of this problem, the British tried to settle Aborigines in protectorates. In *Bringing them Home*, the report on the Stolen Generation, it is recorded that, 'Between 1838 and 1849 Victoria was the site of an unsuccessful "protectorate" experiment in which government appointed protectors attempted to persuade indigenous people to "settle down to a life of farming".' The Stolen Generation was an episode in Australian history where, from 1837, missions established schools attempting to wean the children away from 'tribal influences'.

Although the European settlement of Victoria occurred without government approval or endorsement, the authorities in Sydney eventually gave in and in 1837 the township of Melbourne was surveyed and named. The colony of Victoria was officially proclaimed on 1 July 1851.

DISCOVERY OF GOLD

The population drain from the state due to the gold rush in New South Wales led the Victorian government to offer a cash reward for the discovery of gold. Victoria was subsequently found to have more gold than the other states combined and, within a decade, the state grew to challenge the supremacy of New South Wales.

By November 1851, alluvial gold had been discovered at Clunes, Anderson's Creek, Buninyong, Ballarat, Mount Alexander and Bendigo (known then as Sandhurst). The streets of Melbourne were virtually deserted and by early 1852, ships from all over the world were disgorging eager miners on the wharves of Melbourne.

Cities like Ballarat, Bendigo and Melbourne immediately accumulated great wealth and Melbourne became the financial centre of the country. In the 1850s, the goldfields injected more than £100 million into the economy of Victoria. The government imposed a substantial mining licence fee for which miners had to pay regardless of their success. This

Above: Gold prospectors were attracted to the Australian goldfields from hundreds of different countries. By 1858 Macphersons Store in Bendigo could boast customers from all over the world.

Above: One of Victoria's most impressive tourist attractions is Sovereign Hill at Ballarat where an entire mining township has been recreated.

became a major grievance between government officials and miners. Relations between them reached such a low point that at Ballarat on 3 December 1854 a group of miners, led by Peter Lalor, fought a brief and bloody battle with government forces at the Eureka Stockade. Thirty men were killed and a large number of agitators were subsequently arrested. When they were brought before the courts in Melbourne, juries refused to convict them. The Eureka flag is still a famous symbol of a brief moment when working-class Australians rose up against government authorities.

Above: One of Victoria's popular conservative politicians and premiers was Henry, later Sir Henry, Bolte whose populist appeal was so strong that he was state premier five times.

DEVELOPMENT OF THE STATE

In 1855 a Legislative Council and Legislative Assembly were created to administer the colony. However, membership and voting rights were tied to ownership of substantial tracts of land. Thus, the first parliament was made up almost entirely of lawyers, successful businessmen, affluent squatters and merchants. With a growing population, the Legislative Assembly politicians were flexible enough to introduce a series of reforms. In 1856 the state introduced the secret ballot—possibly the first in the world.

The goldfields had made Victoria the most multicultural colony in Australia. During the 1850s, people from all over the world were drawn to the colony to try their luck. Inevitably this influx produced some conflicts which boiled over with the arrival of the Chinese—who numbered 40 000 by 1858. Victorian miners protested, demanding that the government slow down the rate of Chinese migration. In 1857 at Buckland River, 2500 Chinese were forced off the goldfield by an angry mob of European miners.

When gold mining collapsed in the 1880s and 1890s, the state went through difficult economic times. Victoria tried to encourage miners to stay in the state by successfully offering them incentives to settle and farm the land.

Left: Melbourne's glory days started in the 1860s and consequently the city has some of the finest examples of Victorian architecture of any city in the world. This ornate iron lacework decorates Tasma Terrace, in East Melbourne.

Above: A symbol of Melbourne's sophistication and cultural diversity, Lygon Street with its restaurants and cafes is the city's 'Little Italy'.

POST-WAR MIGRATION

After World War II, Australia campaigned to attract migrants of European descent. Preference was given to British migrants who were offered assisted passages from 1947 until 1972 when the program was expanded. As a result, by the mid-1970s Australia had immigration assistance plans in place with Italy, Greece, Holland, West Germany, Yugoslavia, Poland and Austria. Many migrants from these countries arrived in Victoria.

The post-war immigration boom brought one million migrants to Australia by 1955—many were refugees from war-torn Europe, mainly from Eastern European nations. Migrants in the 1950s and early 1960s came from Mediterranean countries, particularly from Italy and Greece. During the latter period, 70 000 refugees also arrived, including 14 000 Hungarians.

Partly because it has a similar climate to their native countries (Melbourne and Athens are on the same latitude), and partly because it looks and feels more like a European country, the state welcomed the migrants who arrived from Europe. Migrants worked in the new Australian manufacturing sector that arose in Victoria, which could not have functioned without them. The 1960s were a period of great prosperity for Victoria.

Today Victoria is noted for its rich multicultural society. Places like Lygon Street, famed for its international cuisine, are symbols of the colourful cultural diversity of Melbourne. It is often said as a joke, but for many years it was true, that Melbourne had attracted so many Greek migrants that it was the second-largest Greek city in the world. A vibrancy had come to a city which was once noted for its probity and decidedly British values.

A symbol of Victoria's importance, and Melbourne's status, was the first Olympic Games ever held in the southern hemisphere on 22 November 1956. The Melbourne Olympics attracted 67 nations to a series of venues (the main Olympic stadium was the mighty Melbourne Cricket Ground) and a series of now-legendary Australians won a record of thirteen gold medals for their country.

Above: High-rise development characterises Melbourne's central business district which is attractively located on the banks of the Yarra River.

Following pages: The view across Port Phillip from St Kilda Pier looking towards Melbourne's central business district.

Above: The rustic charm of an old shearing shed. There was a time when Victoria rode on the wealth generated by its sheep industry.

VICTORIA TODAY

Modern Victoria is a society which is modern and multicultural while still retaining some vestiges of an historic conservatism. Both the Country Party (now the federal National Party) and the federal Liberal Party found their roots in Victorian society. It is no accident that, although the Liberal Party has had seven Prime Ministers since the World War II, all but two have come from Victoria.

It is equally intriguing that, in the past 30 years, the state has been dominated by larger-than-life Premiers who feel that they have some special place in the larger arena of Australian politics. Henry Bolte, who was Premier from 1955 until his retirement in 1973, was known for his active defence of the state against federal intervention and, in more recent times, Jeff Kennett (who became Premier in 1993) has been critical of the federal government policies.

Today the state's economy derives from rural enterprises (lambs and wool in the west, dairying and timber in the east), brown coal mining in the Latrobe Valley, vast gas and oil

Above: Recognised as the state's premier natural tourist attraction, the Twelve Apostles on the Great Ocean Road are soft limestone stacks weathered by the forces of the Southern Ocean.

Above: The 'Elephants Hide', one of the many dramatic sandstone features in the beautiful Grampians National Park near Halls Gap.

Right: The curiously named 'The Nobbies' at the edge of Phillip Island are home to considerable populations of birds and seals.

reserves off the Gippsland coast, and well-established secondary industries (such as car manufacturing and textiles) around the main centres of Melbourne, Geelong, Ballarat and Bendigo. Tourists can enjoy the remarkable diversity of the state by visiting the beautiful Dandenong Ranges to the east of Melbourne and the extensive grasslands to the north and west. The Great Ocean Road winds 320 kilometres along the coastline and passing small beaches, spectacular headlands, rugged cliffs and the majestic Twelve Apostles. Premier vineyards are established in the Yarra Glen region, and The Grampians, a range of sandstone ridges situated in the Great Dividing Range, is a popular attraction for bushwalkers. The Snowy Mountains to the north of the state are also dotted with popular ski resorts.

Australian Capital Territory

THE FEDERAL CAPITAL

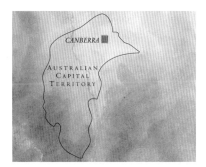

THE FEDERAL CAPITAL

The Australian Capital Territory is the product of historical state rivalry and political compromise between Sydney and Melbourne. Its roots lie in the changing fortunes of the country's two largest cities in the nineteenth century. Effectively, from 1788 until the gold rushes in the 1840s, Sydney was the continent's pre-eminent city. Set on a beautiful harbour, being the first European settlement and the centre of government, it was a natural capital. However, with the gold boom of the 1840s and 1850s and the emergence of the great goldfields at Ballarat, Bendigo and many other gold-mining towns throughout Victoria, Melbourne began to challenge Sydney's 'premier' status. Melbourne was the new 'capital' awash with gold money, affluence and pretension.

EMERGENCE OF THE FEDERAL CAPITAL

During the 1890s, when the discussions about Federation became serious, there was inevitably an enormous amount of competition between Melbourne and Sydney for the position of federal capital. An agreement was finally reached that the capital would be neither Melbourne nor Sydney—instead, a committee would locate a place roughly equidistant between them, the Australian Capital Territory. When the Federation of Australian states was declared in 1901, the search for this location and its name had to begin. Numerous names were suggested, some of them absurd—Sydmelbane being a famous one—and a parliamentary committee headed off around the country to find a suitable location. The committee travelled around New South Wales and inspected various country towns such as Orange, Bathurst and Armidale. Eventually it decided on a small settlement named Canberra in 1909. By 1911 the Australian Capital Territory had been created.

Above: Having won the international competition to design Canberra, the capital city, Walter Burley Griffin emigrated to Australia from the United States.

Opposite: As late as 1913, more than a decade after Federation, the nation's capital was still only sheep paddocks and undulating hills. This view of the national capital was painted by Penleigh Boyd in 1913.

Previous pages: The splendid autumn colours of Canberra.

Above: An early photograph of the area around Canberra (with Black Mountain in the background). No wonder early residents of the national capital thought they were living on a farm.

ABORIGINAL PRESENCE

For thousands of years before the arrival of Europeans, the Australian Capital Territory area, which includes the Southern Highlands and Tablelands, was inhabited by the Ngunawal, Walgalu and Djimantan Aborigines. They lived in relatively small communities hunting goannas, possums, kangaroos and wallabies which they cooked in hot ashes. They adopted burning off practices, as the new shoots which emerged after fire attracted kangaroos. For hunting they used clubs, spears and stone axes made of hard rock bound to a wooden handle.

These Aboriginal groups did not give up the area to the Europeans without a fight. For instance, the Brindabella valley, which lies to the west of Canberra just beyond the boundaries of the Australian Capital Territory, was settled as a stock outstation in the 1830s. However, it was always regarded as a dangerous area and shepherds were afraid to tend their sheep there. In 1849 Joseph Franklin purchased the land and tried to settle in the Brindabella valley but the Aborigines killed his cattle and drove him out. Franklin did not return until 1863, by which time most of the Aborigines had been killed by the gold miners who had poured through the valleys in search of new goldfields beyond Araluen, Kiandra and Adelong.

EUROPEAN SETTLEMENT

The first Europeans arrived in the area in 1820 and these included Dr Charles Throsby, Joseph Wild, James Vaughan and Charles Throsby Smith (Throsby's nephew), who reached Lake George and probably saw the Brindabella Ranges. In October 1820, Charles Throsby brought the Governor of New South Wales, Lachlan Macquarie, to the area and by December, the first Europeans had walked through the valley where Lake Burley Griffin is now located and climbed Black Mountain. The following year Charles Throsby reached Tuggeranong and in 1823 Joshua Moore's 'Canberry' station was established. By 1825 Robert Campbell had settled at Duntroon and a decade later the first Lanyon homestead was built in the Tuggeranong Valley. This was an area of isolated settlers who used the rich pasturelands for grazing. For the first 20 years, life was hard and the settlers had to travel long distances to purchase supplies. A small community had been established by 1845 when St John's Church (which still stands) was completed. Three years later the community had its own school and by the 1860s most of the district had been settled by farmers. The development of the towns in the area was relatively rapid. By 1851 Queanbeyan (which now lies outside the Australian Capital Territory) had a population of 372 and there were probably around 1000 people living in what is now the Australian Capital Territory.

URBAN EXPANSION

If there had been no decision to convert the area into the national capital it is quite likely that it would have remained much like the rest of the district—that is, a few small townships servicing the needs of the larger properties and a number of elegant residences on substantial land holdings. However, with Federation, 2330 square kilometres of good-quality sheep grazing land were carved out of New South Wales in 1908 to form the Australian Capital Territory. As an eccentric afterthought, the Seat of Government Australian Capital Territory (1908) declared that access to the sea was imperative. Thus 7400 hectares of land at the southern end of Jervis Bay were officially handed over from New South Wales to the Commonwealth government to be developed as a port and naval base.

On 1 January 1911, the Australian Capital Territory was officially handed over to the Commonwealth government. That same year a competition was launched for the design of a city for 25 000 people, won by the American Walter Burley Griffin whose design, based on a series of geometrically precise circles and crosses, was similar to the street patterns of Washington and Paris.

Above: Duntroon property was established by Robert Campbell in 1825. The homestead was built soon after and still stands as part of the country's leading military academy in Canberra.

THEIR NAME LIVETH FOR EVERMORE

Above: With its Pool of Reflection and its Roll of Honour which lists 102 000 Australians who have died at war, the Australian War Memorial stands solemnly at the top of Anzac Parade.

Opposite: The Carillon Memorial stands on the edge of Lake Burley Griffin opposite the High Court. When played, the sound of the bells floats across the waters of the lake.

EARLY YEARS

The early years of Canberra's formation could be described as consisting of a few isolated buildings, a lot of hasty building and a lot of politicians feeling as though they really were stuck out in a sheep paddock trying to make decisions about the future of the entire country. When the Prince of Wales (later King Edward VIII) arrived in Canberra in 1920 to lay a foundation stone on Capital Hill, he is said to have remarked that Canberra consisted almost entirely of foundation stones. Government House at Yarralumla had been built in 1891 on land which had been used for sheep grazing since the 1830s. It was purchased by the Commonwealth government in 1911 and was used for the first Cabinet meeting which was held in Canberra on 30 January 1924. The house was subsequently remodelled. The 1920s were really the watershed in the city's history. In 1927 federal parliament officially moved from Melbourne to Canberra. Of course, while the politicians moved the public servants wanted to stay put and it took the next 40 years to move all of the head offices of government departments to Canberra. At the time there was an obvious building boom and much of 'old Canberra' dates from this time. The Prime Minister's Lodge was completed in 1923. The suburbs of Deakin and Forrest, both of which are characterised by full-brick dwellings often with a slight 'Spanish mission' appearance, were completed around this time and designed to house newly arriving public servants. The Hotel Canberra, a beautiful art

Above: The first parliament house in Canberra was completed in 1927 and for sixty-one years it was the hub of the nation's political life. Today it is a pleasant museum and art gallery.

Opposite: Completed and opened in 1988, to celebrate the Bicentenary of European settlement in Australia, the new Parliament House allows the public to stand on top of the politicians.

Following pages: View of Canberra with Black Mountain in the distance.

deco building designed by John Smith Murdoch (he later drew up the plans for Parliament House), was opened in 1924 and instantly became the 'home' of politicians, journalists and public servants. The first Parliament House was started in 1923. At its peak there were 250 men working on the site. It was officially opened by the Duke of York on 9 May 1927.

EXPANSION DURING THE 1960s

Most of the public servants recruited in Sydney or Melbourne did not want to move to a small, isolated 'town' in the middle of nowhere. This was compounded by the fact that many of the head offices of Commonwealth government departments continued to operate out of the state capitals. By the late 1950s, however, a plan was in place to move all the head offices to Canberra. The strategy was careful. First, any person seeking a career with promotion prospects had to move to Canberra. With this came the rapid development of good housing to cater for a variety of public servants. Its education facilities—particularly the excellent high schools and the Australian National University—received large funds to make them some of the best academic institutions in the country. Recruitment of new public servants now actively advocated a move to Canberra. The incentive of rapid promotion was held out while, at the same time, potential public servants were told that the beach (at Batemans Bay) was only two hours drive from the national capital and the 'night

Above: The remarkable Aboriginal memorial, a series of dramatic poles which take up an entire room at the National Art Gallery.

life' was attractive and dynamic. This resulted in the rapid construction of two satellite areas—Woden Valley and Tuggeranong—which grew rapidly and provided low-cost housing for people drawn to the new and expanding city. To understand its expansion, the population in 1947 was only 15 156. By 1962, it was 64 000 and today it is Australia's eighth-largest city with a population in excess of 300 000.

CANBERRA TODAY

Canberra is a city where the 'frontier' nature of the typical Australian town—gawdy service stations, roads without curbs and proper guttering, neon signs and casual development—has been replaced with planning and precision. It has the best roads and cycleways, the most discreet shopping centres, and attractive tree-lined streets. It is a city which looks cared for. Yet, for all its symmetrical beauty, Canberra lacks something—the element of surprise and spontaneity. The great cities of the world such as those in Europe and Asia have evolved in response to people's needs and are constantly changing. Canberra, however, has been imposed on an environment. The result is a highly structured city surrounded by suburbs. More derogatory comments have been made about Canberra than any national capital deserves. Percy Deane, secretary to the Prime Minister's Department under Billy Hughes, declared that the best view of Canberra was 'from the back of a departing train'. One of the early parliamentarians suggested that it was nothing more than a sheep paddock, and Elspeth Huxley, sister of writer Aldous Huxley, described it as the most middle-class city in the world. Don Dunstan, a former Premier of South Australia, astutely captured a widespread Australian view of the national capital when he observed 'Canberra has such great potential

beauty. But something is lacking. The city is like a woman expensively coiffured, dressed and made-up, well-educated, courteous—and frigid. Canberra boasts more than a million trees and shrubs, but many are exotics and most are neatly regimented. Pretty, but it could be a city of anywhere. When you sit up in the Lakeside Hotel and look out at the nightscape, the only thing seemingly missing is Flash Gordon whizzing around the curve below. But what is really missing is any feeling of Australia.'

Despite its shortcomings, Canberra today is a city of great aesthetic beauty with broad roadways, superb parklands and many elegant buildings. On a clear spring or autumn day, it is a city which is captivating in its graciousness. Events like the spectacular floral display Floriade held each spring highlight the natural beauties of the city. The views across Lake Burley Griffin are breathtaking, while from the War Memorial it is possible to look across to the elegant new Parliament House on Capital Hill. From the shores of the lake, the reflections of buildings such as the High Court and the National Library are exceptional.

Above: Each spring Canberra's parks and gardens burst into spectacular displays of colour and the Floriade Festival attracts thousands of visitors to the city.

QUEENSLAND

THE SUNSHINE STATE

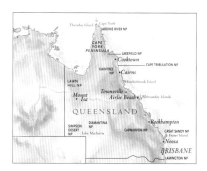

THE SUNSHINE STATE

Above: John Oxley, who reached and explored the Brisbane River in 1823 and returned to establish a colony the following year, was the founding father of the city of Brisbane.

Opposite: Early Brisbane may have been a prosperous colonial outpost but its prosperity hid the dispossession of the local Aborigines with the arrival of Europeans.

Previous pages: Lady Musgrave Island, a true coral cay on Queensland's Great Barrier Reef.

Containing the second-largest land area of the Australian states and territories within its borders, Queensland's natural environmental wonders, such as intense tracks of tropical rainforests and the Great Barrier Reef World Heritage area, commingle with its traditional history of exploration, mining and farming.

It is a state which started life as a centre for sheep and cattle and which, in the past 40 years, has become Australia's premier holiday destination. Given the number of major tourist attractions it offers, it is hardly surprising that a recent survey of visitors from overseas found that more than 60 per cent nominated Queensland as their primary destination in Australia. Where else in the world is there a reef formation over 1000 kilometres long? Where else can you laze on a tropical beach only moments away from modern urban society? Where else can you see troupes of Aboriginal actors and dancers re-enact the stories of their Dreaming? Where else can you drive for hours across an ancient seabed seeing nothing but the occasional emu and forlorn mobs of sheep?

A RICH ARCHAEOLOGICAL HISTORY

It is now known that Aborigines moved into Queensland about 50 000 years ago, moving across from Western Australia and the Northern Territory where they had landed some 5000 to 10 000 years earlier. The most important archaeological find in the state was at Kenniff Cave in 1962 when tools dating from 16 000 years ago were discovered. Subsequent digs at the cave have taken this date back to about 19 000 years ago and demonstrated two clearly defined periods in the development of stone tools.

Above: Macassan traders, now part of Indonesia, came to the Australian coast to collect and purchase sea cucumbers (bêche de mer) to sell in China.

Archaeological finds have revealed much about prehistoric Queensland. The finds at Lark Quarry Environmental Park (near Winton in western Queensland), which are some 95 million years old, include the largest group of footprints of running dinosaurs uncovered anywhere in the world. In the town of Hughenden the remains of a large land dinosaur from 100 million years ago, the Muttaburrasaurus.

EXPLORATION AND EUROPEAN SETTLEMENT

In 1606 the Dutch sailor Willem Janszoon, captaining the *Duyfken*, landed on the western coast of Cape York in north Queensland—but he did not know he was on Australian soil.

Both the Europeans and Macassans (Indonesian fishermen) explored the western coast of Cape York and in 1770 Captain James Cook sailed up the east coast of Australia. Trying to chart his way through the Great Barrier Reef proved impossible and, as a result of the reef, Cook ran aground and was forced to drag his boat for repairs into the estuary of the Endeavour River at the present-day site of Cooktown. It was here that the first European settlement of Queensland, and indeed of Australia, occurred.

Matthew Flinders, circumnavigating Australia in 1799, sailed up the coast carefully charting the reef and the coastline as he went. A more comprehensive survey of the Great Barrier Reef occurred between 1802 and 1850 when a variety of adventurers and explorers, including Philip King (1815) and Owen Stanley (1848), tentatively made their way through the shoals, atolls, coral cays and danger zones which characterised the region.

Land exploration began in the 1820s. In 1823, John Oxley travelled north discovering the Tweed River (now on the New South Wales–Queensland border), and in November he reached the waters of Moreton Bay. Within days of his arrival he came upon three escaped convicts—Thomas Pamphlett, Richard Parsons and John Finnegan—who claimed that while on a wood-cutting expedition they had been swept out to sea, floating north and eventually ending up on Moreton Island. They had been found by Aborigines who had shown them the local source of fresh water. Oxley named it the Brisbane River after the Governor. That same year, the explorer Allan Cunningham had reached Cunningham's Gap and the rich Darling Downs, but the government resisted free settlement in this area until 1842, resulting in a boom for the Queensland area (still part of New South Wales).

Sugar cane was planted along the coast and dairy and beef cattle were overlanded to properties stretching from the Darling Downs to the Atherton Tableland in the far north. The aggressive north-bound push of pastoralists, with their substantial production of wool, hides and tallow, forced the creation of a number of ports on the coast.

The pastoralists encouraged European exploration. Most admired was the German explorer Ludwig Leichhardt, who organised a party in 1844 to travel from Jimbour Station (230 kilometres north-west of Brisbane) to Port Essington in the Northern Territory. The party arrived exhausted at Port Essington in December 1845. When they finally returned to Sydney in 1846, Leichhardt was greeted as a hero and hailed as the 'Prince of Explorers'.

The settlers in Queensland were met with unprecedented levels of resistance from the local Aborigines and it is said that Queensland's frontier life was more dangerous than anywhere else. Today it is still possible to visit Old Rainworth Station near the Carnarvon Ranges and see holes in the side of the house which were used as rifle points when Aborigines attacked—which they did regularly.

Many Aborigines attempted to help the European explorers. The most famous example is the fateful journey of Robert O'Hara Burke and Williams Wills who, in 1860, travelled from Melbourne to the Gulf of Carpentaria, driven by wanting to be the first to cross the continent. Burke and Wills died on this journey in spite of assistance from the local Aborigines. In their wake came William Landsborough, Frederick Walker and John McKinlay, all looking for the explorers. Ironically, as a by-product of their search they discovered both the pastoral and mining potential of the Gulf.

Above: Conscripted labour (known as kanakas), mostly from the islands of the South Pacific, came to Queensland to work in the sugar cane fields.

Above: The narrow coastal strip from Brisbane to Port Douglas is agriculturally rich. Here sugar cane fields nestle under the mountains of the Great Dividing Range.

GOLD RUSHES AND LAND GRABS

In the 1870s and 1880s there was a 'land grab' in far western Queensland, with pastoralists claiming huge areas of the land that they stocked with cattle. This pastoral industry was the basis of Queensland's economic success for nearly a century until the decline of the beef and wool industry in the 1960s.

The last great gold rushes in Australia occurred in Queensland in the 1870s and 1880s when gold was discovered at Gympie, along the Palmer River and in a number of locations on the Atherton Tablelands. The subsequent gold rushes opened up some of the state's most inhospitable countryside, with miners arriving in frontier port towns like Cooktown and Port Douglas. Townsville, Cardwell, Port Douglas, Cairns and Cooktown all started life as ports from which gold could be shipped out. The real challenge for the miners was finding routes from the tablelands down the steep escarpment to these ports—they had to deal with sheer cliffs, dense rainforest and hostile Aborigines.

Around this time there was also a push to use the coastal hinterland for sugar production. Sugar all over the world was being harvested by cheap black labourers from the

South Pacific, known as 'kanakas', who were treated like virtual slaves. Consequently towns like Innisfail, Ingham and Mourilyan were established around the sugar mills.

VALUE OF MINING

Since the 1960s, Queensland has been increasingly dependent on its mining industry as a source of wealth. The state has huge reserves of coking and steaming coal that are mined by open-cut methods in the region to the west of the huge coal terminal at Gladstone.

The other major area of mineral discovery has been oil. In 1961, crude oil was discovered at Moonie in the state's south-east and more recently, large deposits of natural gas have added to this rich power source.

Equally important was the discovery of bauxite at Weipa. It wasn't until 1955, when geologist Harry Evans realised that the 'reddish cliffs' were virtually pure bauxite, that the potential of the area began to be exploited. The result is that Weipa is now the largest bauxite mine in the world. In fact, the state is so rich in minerals that, depending on the world prices and demand, gold and silver mines are regularly opened and shut down.

Above: Townsville. Gold prospectors flocked to north Queensland arriving along the coast from Townsville to Cooktown before heading inland to the gold diggings at Ravenswood.

Above: Surfers Paradise, the prime holiday destination on the long strip of beaches known as the Gold Coast.

Opposite: The Great Barrier Reef stretches for over 2000 kilometres and has an amazing variety of coral and fish.

Following pages: Lawn Hill National Park has sheer 60-metre sandstone walls amid lush tropical vegetation.

TOURISM

By the turn of the century the coastal areas, particularly those within easy reach of Brisbane and the southern states, were becoming important tourist destinations. The modern Gold Coast was created by Jim Cavill who in 1933 renamed the coastal town of Elston to Surfers Paradise, building a hotel with a small zoo and a huge beer garden.

The potential of the Great Barrier Reef as a tourist attraction began to be realised around the 1950s so that, by the 1980s, the state's economy was largely driven by coastal tourism. In 1992, the coast boasted over 60 international hotels and tourist resorts, more than a dozen huge marinas, and a network of ancillary facilities such as casinos, charter cruises, sporting complexes, and hundreds of motels and restaurants.

QUEENSLAND TODAY

Modern-day Queensland with its capital, Brisbane, consists of competing interests. Historically the state was created and nurtured by agriculture. The inland and the highlands, notably the Atherton Tablelands, were ideal for beef and sheep. The coastal waters are rich with fish and crustaceans, the slopes of the Great Dividing Range were an important source of valuable tropical timber (however, Queensland is now a net importer of timber), and the alluvial coastal plains were an ideal growing environment for tropical crops. Consequently, the state has always been administered with an eye on the power of the rural lobby.

Recently, however, the power of the pastoralists has been challenged by coastal developers and Native Title legislation, which in turn are challenged by conservation and

Above: The magnificent view along the Brisbane River from the city's beautiful Botanic Gardens.

Opposite: The highlight of Mount Coot-tha Botanical Gardens is the unusual Tropical Dome indoor display with its thousands of tropical plants.

Above: Inland Queensland is a vast flat region characterised by grasslands and cattle country.

Right: The north Queensland coast is a rich area of tropical rainforest where plants like the strangler fig thrive.

preservation lobbyists wanting to preserve the state's spectacular environmental assets. Tourism development has not occurred without its critics. Environmentalists have long waged campaigns to protect the coastline and its wetlands from development.

Above all, Queensland is a truly wonderful region of Australia, boasting the warmest, most perfect weather. Its diversity is breathtaking and its beauty, particularly in the rainforest regions, in its coastal beaches and in its seemingly infinite outback plains, lives in the memory of travellers long after their journeys are over.

TASMANIA

THE APPLE ISLE

THE APPLE ISLE

In a very real sense, Tasmania is totally different from the rest of Australia, being wet and cold while the mainland is predominantly hot and dry, and having rolling hills and green valleys while the mainland is flat and expansive. In the past, the community's belief in the need to maintain industry in order to survive has meant that huge dams were built, largely by post-war emigrants, as an incentive to attract business wanting cheap power. Tasmania's landscape has been further decimated by polluting mills, mining and logging. However, Tasmania's dependence on using natural resources for commerce, at the expense of its environmental assets, is slowly decreasing.

Historically, in so many ways, Tasmania has always been unique from mainland Australia. When Sydney Town was thriving, the settlement at Hobart Town was struggling. When the vast grazing lands of eastern Australia were being opened up, Tasmanians were struggling with small acreages between Hobart and George Town. When New South Wales and Victoria were getting rich as a result of the gold discoveries, Tasmania was teetering on the edge of a depression. The combination of Bass Strait (a formidable barrier), a history of hardship, a small population and a fragile economic base has seen the state struggle in its development. However, many people appreciate the state's uniqueness. A careful mixture of tourism (particularly eco-tourism) and boutique wineries and farms as sources of revenue, and a desire by many people to seek a peaceful, more tranquil kind of life, have increased Tasmania's population in recent years. Its spectacular wilderness, quaint Georgian villages and fascinating colonial history reflect the natural splendour and diversity of this state. From its origins as a destination for convicts, Tasmania presents itself today as a state with a confident self-identity.

Above: The great Dutch sailor Abel Tasman first sighted Van Diemen's Land in 1642.

Opposite: Located on the Derwent River, Hobart Town was known for its hardship and the toughness of its residents.

Previous pages: Lake Hanson, Cradle Mountain National Park.

Above: The remarkable Truganini, probably the last full-blooded Tasmanian Aborigine, died in Hobart in 1876 having witnessed the genocide of her people.

A RICH ARCHAEOLOGICAL HISTORY

It is believed that the Aborigines who arrived in Northern Australia about 60 000 years ago reached Tasmania around 30 000 years ago, when it was still linked to the mainland (geological evidence suggests that the sea level at the time was 120 metres lower than it is today). Ice Age Aborigines would have travelled to Tasmania via a land bridge which lay to the east of present-day Melbourne. The bridge seems to have continued to exist until about 12 000 years ago when sea levels rose and those Aborigines living on Tasmania were effectively cut off from continuous contact with the mainland.

Tasmania's Aborigines survived, removed from their neighbours to the north, for nearly 12 000 years. They were efficient in their hunting and were well prepared for the coldness of the winters using animal fat to protect their bodies and making large coats from the hides of animals. Tragically, it was also their isolation that made them so ill-equipped for the invasion which occurred in the early years of the nineteenth century.

There have been major ancient archaeological discoveries in Tasmania, the most important of which is at Fraser Cave on the banks of the lower Franklin River in 1977. Subsequent investigation revealed, as the archaeologist Rhys Jones noted, 'that the whole site could have the order of 10 to 100 million artefacts in it and that makes it one of the richest sites ever found in Australia'.

DISCOVERY AND CONFLICT

The first European to reach Tasmania was the Dutch navigator and explorer, Abel Tasman. Sailing from Batavia (Java) he landed on the east coast of Tasmania in 1642 and, not knowing he was on an island, took possession of the land.

No further exploration of the island took place for the next 130 years. Then, in quick succession, the island was visited by Marion du Fresne (1772), Furneaux (1773), Cook (1777), Bligh (1788), J.H. Cox (1789), Bruni d'Entrecasteaux and Huon de Kermadec (1792–93), and John Hayes (1793). During 1798 and 1799, Bass and Flinders circumnavigated the island. It was around this time that the island became popular with whalers and sealers. They were the first to exploit the indigenous population, the beginning of a process which wiped out all the full-blood Aborigines and left only a tiny community of mixed-blood people to remind the world that once the island had been inhabited by a peaceful group of people. The atrocities against the Aborigines during the first 20 to 30 years of the nineteenth century can be symbolically summed up in the life of Truganini, the much-

abused and resilient Aboriginal woman who was to be incorrectly dubbed 'the last of her tribe'. Truganini died in 1876 in Hobart, but her skeleton was not cremated until 1976.

By 1818 the Aboriginal population of the island had fallen from 4000 to below 2000. In 1838 there were 90 left, and by 1876 they had all died. Today a small number of descendants of sealers and Aboriginal women still live in Tasmania.

Above: Port Arthur, a vast penal colony, was built to the east of Hobart Town. Between 1830 and 1877 it was home to some 12500 convicts.

EUROPEAN SETTLEMENT AND CONVICT LABOUR

The formal European settlement of Van Diemen's Land occurred in 1804 when the British authorities, concerned about French interests in the region, decided to assert their rights over the island. Between March 1803 and June 1804, convicts, soldiers and free settlers arrived at Risdon Cove and Sullivans Cove on the Derwent River. The settlement was named Hobart Town. The early history of the settlement was characterised by extreme hardship and constant skirmishes with Aborigines.

Later in 1804 a settlement was established on the north coast at George Town at the mouth of the Esk River. In 1806 the settlement was moved further south to the present site of Launceston and by 1812, the two major settlements of Hobart and Launceston were being jointly run by a single administration.

The life of convicts on Van Diemen's Land was harsh. Perhaps the most unforgiving of all of the penal settlements was that established on Sarah Island in Macquarie Harbour on

Above: The four-storey sandstone Penitentiary at Port Arthur was reputedly the largest building in Australia when it was completed in 1844.

the island's west coast. The terrain around it is cold-climate rainforest, the entrance to the harbour is narrow and dangerous, and the waves braking on the shores beyond the entrance to the harbour have a clear run from the south pole. Convicts rowed up to 20 miles a day from the penal camp at Sarah Island to Gordon River where they felled Huon pine (a beautiful, ancient and now rare and cherished wood) for the construction of ships.

On the eastern side of the island, life for convicts at the famous Port Arthur penal site bordered on slavery. For example, a railway line ran from Port Arthur to the jetty at Little Norfolk Bay, which was designed to carry passengers and supplies from the security of Norfolk Bay across the narrow isthmus to Port Arthur and Long Bay. The railway, the first in Australia, used four convicts to push the carriages along the seven-kilometre line.

The most important work performed by convict gangs in the early nineteenth century was the building of a series of elegant stone villages (including some particularly impressive bridges and churches) along the route from Hobart to Launceston. Today villages like Richmond and Ross bear witness to their work. In fact, the bridge at Ross is the third-oldest bridge still standing in Australia and is recognised as the most important convict-built bridge in the country.

Above: Throughout Tasmania, from Sarah Island on the west coast to Saltwater River on the east coast, the visitor will find ruins which are stark reminders of the island's early history.

Following pages: The coastline along the edge of the Freycinet National Park, on the east coast of Tasmania, is characterised by rugged granite outcrops and mountains.

DEVELOPMENT OF THE APPLE ISLE

The state's early governors struggled to manage a colony which was expanding rapidly with new landowners; although, by the 1830s, when the economy was relatively stable, settlers still had to grapple with high interest rates and a shortage of currency. A sudden boom in land prices in the late 1830s led to a depression in the 1840s, which was exacerbated by too much spare convict labour. By 1852 the island had a representative council and the British parliament agreed that transportation of convicts would cease the following year. In 1855 the name was changed from Van Diemen's Land to Tasmania.

The state's economy suffered further until the 1870s because wages fell, crops failed and labourers were left to try their luck on the Victorian goldfields. This period of economic downturn was only relieved when tin was discovered. Although the island's rugged west coast made access difficult, gold was subsequently found along the Pieman River, silver was found at Waratah, Zeehan, Dundas and Farrell, copper was mined at Mount Lyell, and tin at Renison Bell. From 1871 to 1891, the island's population rose from 99 000 to 146 000. The mining boom flowed onto other industries such as fruit and wool, but World War I drew men away and the short post-war boom did not bring a significant return in population.

Above: On a map Tasmania looks like an apple. It is entirely appropriate then that one of its most important industries should be apple growing and the processing of apple byproducts.

Opposite: Tasmania has always had a delicate economy. The commercial growing of lavender has offered the island both work and much-needed income.

Above: The valley which stretches through the centre of the island from Hobart to Launceston is rich, fertile and ideal for the grazing of beef and dairy cattle.

SEARCH FOR A MODERN ECONOMIC BASE

The island was (and still is) famous for both its excellent dairy products and its extensive stands of timber, particularly of the valuable Huon pine. These primary products ensured that the island enjoyed reasonable economic stability, which were enriched by mining and fruit industries. The early century saw the establishment of an electrolytic zinc works at Risdon (1917), and in the late 1930s–early 1940s, Tasmania started to cut down hardwoods for the paper mills, which were established in Burnie (1938) and Boyer (1941). The state's abundant power attracted an aluminium smelter at Bell Bay (1955), another paper manufacturing plant at Wesley Vale (1971) and a woodchip mill at Long Reach (1972). Unfortunately these industries were later vulnerable to global stockmarkets. However, in recent years, boutique industries have arisen with the successful cultivation and exportation of lavender, flowers, grapes, olives, walnuts and Asian vegetables to foreign markets, becoming major contributions to Tasmania's economy today.

HYDRO-ELECTRICITY

As a panacea to the state's economic woes, the government succeeded in attracting industry to the state by selling cheap power; but, while the hydro power itself was 'clean', the industries that arrived were not. They created large amounts of coastal and river pollution.

The first hydro scheme, known as Waddamana, started in 1911 and was completed in 1916. In the early 1960s, the waters of the Great Lake were diverted through Poatina and Trevallyn power stations, and in 1973, a scheme involving the Mersey and Forth rivers was completed. The next plan involved the Gordon, Serpentine and Huon rivers in south-western Tasmania. This area was characterised by wilderness and, when the project was completed, it drowned Lake Pedder, noted for its exceptional beauty, and Lake Gordon.

Above: One of Tasmania's premier tourist attractions is the exceptionally beautiful Lake St Clair National Park where the Cradle Mountain Lake attracts thousands of sightseers and bushwalkers each year. It was saved from exploitation for hydro-electricity. Sadly many equally beautiful lakes were drowned to form catchments for dams which became part of the state's hydro-electricity grid.

*Above: Typical of Tasmania—
the intimate beauty of the Liffey Falls
near the historic village of Deloraine.*

*Opposite: The spectacularly glaciated
western and central regions of
Tasmania include the beautiful
Lake Oberon, part of the island's
pristine wilderness.*

The Hydro-Electric Commission planned to build a dam and power station on the Gordon River, but they were opposed by conservation groups who organised a series of effective nationwide protests. The result was that in 1982 the Commonwealth government had the whole area listed as World Heritage and, in 1983, the new Labor government of Bob Hawke legislated to prevent the development of the project.

TASMANIA TODAY

Since being under the national spotlight with the hydro-electric dam debate, Tasmania began to promote its rugged topography and its outstanding World Heritage wilderness areas—ironically once despised by settlers and used to the advantage of the convicts' gaolers during the 1800s—to become a favourite tourist destination. Its famous fauna, such as the Tasmanian Devil, its ancient flora and its preserved history, combined with its wild, natural environment, make it one of the most beautiful states of Australia.

SOUTH AUSTRALIA

THE FESTIVAL STATE

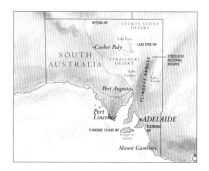

THE FESTIVAL STATE

Historically, South Australia is different to the other Australian states: it was never a penal colony and its earliest European settlers included a substantial number of non-British refugees from Silesia in Prussia. Its capital city, Adelaide, has a gracefulness and elegance which are the product of a careful street plan rather than some hastily constructed penal camp, and the state's reputation for fine wines has resulted from the labours of those Silesian Lutherans who developed the vineyards around Adelaide.

DISCOVERY AND COASTAL EXPLORATION

Prior to European settlement Aborigines were well established throughout South Australia. Although over two-thirds of the state is desert, they adapted their lifestyles and were equipped to live successfully on both the harsh, dry Nullarbor Plain and the temperate well-watered areas around the Murray River.

The first Europeans to sight the coast of South Australia were the Dutch sailors on the *Gulden Zeepaard* who in 1627 sailed along the southern coast of what was then called New Holland and reached the area around Ceduna in South Australia before turning back and making their way north to Batavia (Java). Remarkably, South Australia then remained unexplored until 1792 when the French explorer Bruni d'Entrecasteaux sailed into the Great Australian Bight searching for the French explorer, La Pérouse. He was followed in 1800 by Lieutenant James Grant and in 1802 by Matthew Flinders who, during his circumnavigation of Australia, charted much of the future state's coastline and also discovered Kangaroo Island.

Above: Matthew Flinders, circum-navigated the entire Australian continent in the early years of the 19th century, and explored every bay and headland of the South Australian coastline.

Opposite: Colonel Light constructed a city on the plains which was like a beautiful geometry lesson.

Previous pages: These vineyards, near Tanunda in the heart of the Barossa Valley produce some of the state's most exceptional wines.

Above: Colonel William Light was the creator of Adelaide. He designed the city along a clearly defined grid pattern with the two major centres—Adelaide Central and North Adelaide— surrounded by parklands.

The first official settlement of Kangaroo Island occurred in 1836 when the South Australia Land Company established a base at Nepean Bay. This eventually grew into the island's main town, Kingscote. By 1837, shiploads of German immigrants were being brought to the Island by the South Australia Land Company, but the soil was infertile and the water supply unreliable so that by 1840 the settlement had collapsed and most of the settlers had moved to the mainland.

EUROPEAN SETTLEMENT

The effective European settlement of South Australia was a product of the social idealism of Edward Gibbon Wakefield, a social reformer from Britain. By the 1830s, the Industrial Revolution was causing extraordinary hardship in Britain—overcrowding, extreme poverty and crime. Wakefield, in response to this, challenged the idea that colonies like New South Wales were only good as dumping grounds for Britain's criminals and instead advanced a scheme where the money raised from the sale of Crown land could be invested in the cost of shipping labourers to work on the newly privatised land. Here was a plan for the development of Australia which did not rely on convict labour.

In the early stages it seemed that bureaucracy would ensure that it failed. However, in May 1835, ten commissioners were appointed to oversee the sale of land in the new colony of South Australia. They needed to sell £35 000-worth of land to ensure the colony's success. Within a year, eight ships departed from England bound for the shores of South Australia. By March 1837 the site of Adelaide had been surveyed and land allotted.

By December 1837 explorers were traversing the land beyond Adelaide. On 13 December 1837, the Surveyor-General Colonel William Light travelled into the rich region which would eventually be known as the Barossa Valley and recorded: 'At length about five o'clock we came to a beautiful valley which I named Lynedoch Vale after my much esteemed friend, Lord Lynedoch.' By 1839 Colonel Light was selling off large tracts of land in the valley. It looked as though the colony would be a success. Livestock and settlers were pouring into South Australia and there was a sense of entrepreneurial enthusiasm in the air. Unfortunately, the optimism was short-lived. The new settlers were not hard-working labourers but land speculators. They bought their land and waited for the value to increase so they could sell and make a quick profit.

Fortunately the people who believed in the colony were tireless in their determination to settle the area. A local landowner and director of the South Australia Land Company, George Fife Angas, went to London to try and promote colonisation. While he was there he

met Pastor August Ludwig Christian Kavel who was trying to organise for Lutherans from Silesia (who were being persecuted by the King of Prussia, Friedrich Wilhelm III) to emigrate. Angas was moved by the plight of the Lutherans and not only persuaded Kavel that South Australia was a suitable place to immigrate to but also financially assisted the journey.

The first German settlers arrived on 25 November 1838 at the unfortunately named Port Misery. These settlers established distinctly German villages at several sites, most famously, Hahndorf. In its early years, a town like Tanunda in the heart of the Barossa Valley was the very essence of German Lutheranism. This was far removed from the Anglo-Saxon, British settlements which characterised the rest of the continent.

But the colony's progress was not without its problems. By 1840 there were 14 000 people in the colony and the government was effectively bankrupt. Money had been poorly spent, only 7500 labourers had been sent to the colony, and there were accusations of serious financial mismanagement.

By 1842, the British government had deemed the experiment a failure and South Australia had reverted to an ordinary Crown colony, whereby its administration and laws were governed by the British Crown. This led to a remarkable turnaround. Two years later under the governorship of Captain George Grey, the colony had resolved its financial problems and the farmers (landowners who, in many instances, had been persuaded to go

Above: South Australians are hugely proud that they are the only state in Australia not to be first settled by convicts. They are a true state of free settlers.

Above: John McDouall Stuart's route from South Australia to Darwin was so precise and sensible that it became the route for the Overland Telegraph, the railway line and the road in later years.

Opposite: All of northern and north-western South Australia is nothing more than vast tracts of desert charac-terised by sand dunes and harsh terrain extending to the horizon.

and work their land) were actually producing more wheat than the colony could use. Still, the economy was extremely fragile. It expanded rapidly in the 1840s when silver was discovered near Adelaide and huge copper deposits (a continuing source of wealth for the state) were located near Kapunda and further north at Burra. This mining activity saw an influx of mines, and by 1850 the population of South Australia had grown to 64 000.

DEVELOPMENT OF THE STATE

The discovery of gold in New South Wales and Victoria had a devastating effect on the state. Within two years the colony's population dropped by 25 per cent as men rushed to the goldfields. In order to counteract this population drain, the colony's parliament created the *Bullion Act* which encouraged successful miners to bring their wealth back to South Australia.

The return of the miners brought pressure to change the government structure. In 1850 Britain established two elected houses of parliament to administer the colony, resulting in a new constitution for South Australia which was widely regarded as the most forward-looking and democratic in the British Empire. Unfortunately the constitution was not accompanied by the establishment of political parties and, with independents dominating, the power base changed at least 37 times in the next 33 years.

The economic history of South Australia has been erratic. In the 1860s, spurred on by the success which followed the gold rushes, the state prospered. John McDouall Stuart became the first European to cross the continent from south to north. In the process he opened up valuable grazing lands in the north of the state and huge copper reserves were found at Moonta. South Australia gained control of the Northern Territory in 1863 and the state's human and sheep populations nearly doubled in the decade. This prosperity collapsed with the depression of the 1880s when the state's population growth slowed and its agricultural productivity, hit by drought, was greatly reduced.

By the late 1880s, vast reserves of silver, lead and zinc had been found at Broken Hill. Although the mine was in New South Wales, the economic benefits flowed into South Australia where huge treatment works were constructed at Port Pirie, bringing work and prosperity to the area. Combined with this windfall, the state committed itself to expanding arable agricultural land through such land management practices as the use of superphosphates and the clearing of marginal swamp land, as well as the establishment of communities along the Murray River. Iron ore was discovered to the west of Port Augusta at Iron Knob and a steelworks was built at Whyalla. Economic prosperity was maintained through to the Great Depression.

DETERMINATION TO REBUILD

After World War I, the state actively settled returned soldiers on the Murray River flood plains and Adelaide grew rapidly. Following World War II, the state's fragile economy was sustained by a series of huge projects such as the Morgan–Whyalla pipeline, the Whyalla steelworks and ship building yard, and the Mannum pipeline bringing water from the Murray River to Adelaide. The city of Elizabeth, named after the Queen, was created in 1955. Oil refineries, cheap electricity, munitions factories and successful mining operations boosted the state's economy, but made it vulnerable to international commodity prices.

The most important economic developments came when, in 1963, Santos Ltd found natural gas at Gidgealpa east of the Birdsville Track, and two years on, both oil and gas were discovered at Moomba. In the 1970s, pipelines to both Sydney and Adelaide were opened.

But perhaps the greatest mineral find in South Australia's history was the discovery of one of the world's largest uranium deposits at Roxby Downs Station in 1976. With an estimated 500 000 tonnes of uranium, the mine is currently valued at $60 000 million.

Above: Opal mining around Coober Pedy leaves the landscape looking more like a moon desert than a place on earth.

Opposite: The pleasure cruiser, Murray Princess, now plies the Murray River where once paddlesteamers brought wool from the vast sheep properties of New South Wales and Queensland.

Following pages: The Flinders Ranges, with its beautiful ghost gums and hauntingly blue mountains, are part of the Australian consciousness.

Above: The impossibly flat plains around Maralinga were the site of early atomic tests. At the time no-one cared that these lands were home to Aborigines who had learnt to live in such harsh terrain.

ROCKETS AND NUCLEAR TESTS

In 1946—after the end of World War II—the Australian government received a formal request from Britain to establish a rocket range. As a result of German rocket attacks during the war, the British had decided they needed a rocket-testing range, and the isolation of Woomera in South Australia, combined with its proximity to the railway siding at Pimba, made it an ideal location. Woomera was established as a township in 1948 by the Australian government. The aim was that it would become a base for service and scientific personnel who were working at the Weapons Research Establishment. The area was ideal for space research. The weather was perfect, the atmosphere was dry, most of the days were sunny, and the sky was clear for long periods. By 1964 Woomera had reached a point where research had converted it into a working missile station. In 1966 rockets which were part of the European ELDO space program were launched, followed by the first Australian satellite. In 1969 the personnel associated with the Joint Australian United States Defence Space Communications Station at Nurrungar, only 16 kilometres away, moved into the town.

In 1955 the centre of Maralinga in the inhospitable western desert was established for British nuclear testing. A year later, more nuclear tests were carried out at Emu. The whole area was seen as a treeless, stony desert, deemed to be both uninhabited and uninhabitable.

WINE BY THE BARREL

In contrast to the arid interior, the earliest settlers recognised that the Mediterranean-style climate of southern South Australia was ideal for vineyards, and by as early as 1837, John Barton Hack had planted grapevines at Chichester Gardens in North Adelaide. Today South Australia boasts no fewer than 150 wineries, most of which are located in 13 major areas. The vineyards produce many styles of wine, from cheap cask wines to gold-medal award-winning vintages, and from reds to whites, champagnes, sauternes, ports and sherries.

SOUTH AUSTRALIA TODAY

Over the past 30 years, South Australia has carefully fostered a self-image of being a sophisticated and international cultural centre. During the 1960s, when the rest of Australia was in the thrall of post-Menzies conservatism, its Premier at the time, Don Dunstan, introduced a series of liberal reforms, even symbolically dragging Australian males out of heavy suits and ties by appearing on the steps of Parliament House in pink shorts. During his premiership, the Adelaide Arts Festival, now the pre-eminent national cultural event, was established. The equally daring experiment of providing government funds for the revitalised Australian film industry, nurtured through the South Australian Film

Above: South Australia is famous for its vineyards and wineries with wines from the Adelaide Hills, Barossa Valley, Coonawarra district, Clare Valley and McLaren Vale being internationally honoured.

Above: The River Torrens cuts through Adelaide with the city's central business district and Cultural Centre being reflected in its peaceful waters.

Opposite: Remarkable Rocks, a prominent landmark on the western edge of Kangaroo Island.

Corporation, helped to make possible such films as *Sunday Too Far Away*, *Storm Boy*, *Blue Fin* and *Breaker Morant*. The current Australian film industry owes its very existence to the success and commitment of that South Australian Film Corporation.

Because it cannot compete economically with the larger eastern states, South Australia promotes itself as a centre of fine food, outstanding wines and excellent artistic activity. This has resulted in the state establishing a reputation for being progressive, modern and innovative. The state's major 'cultural' and tourist attractions—the Adelaide Hills, the McLaren Vale, the Barossa and Clare Valley wineries—are all easily located within an hour's drive of Adelaide, while just offshore tranquil Kangaroo Island is a popular escape from the mainland.

WESTERN AUSTRALIA

THE WILDFLOWER STATE

THE WILDFLOWER STATE

Western Australia is called the Wildflower State for good reason. After winter rains, the vast, arid land of Australia's largest state is host to over 8000 species of wildflowers, which is more species than the rest of the world put together. It combines its rich history of Aboriginal occupation, farming and mining with the contrasts of stunning beaches along its coastline, and the unique landforms of some of the oldest areas in the world in the Kimberley and Pilbara regions. Even its sheer size and sense of isolation contribute to making it a spectacular state.

A RICH ARCHAEOLOGICAL HISTORY

The early Aboriginal history of Western Australia is more comprehensive than it is in most other states. The oldest known tools to be discovered anywhere in Australia probably date from around 38 000 years ago and were found in the upper reaches of the Swan River. The area around the Swan River, where most West Australians now live, was also probably favoured by the Aborigines because of its reliable water source and abundant wildlife.

There is archaeological evidence which suggests that around 28 000 years ago Aborigines were living around Devil's Lair, and around 20 000 years ago there were Aborigines on the Nullarbor Plain and at Mount Newman in the Pilbara. Koonalda Cave on the Nullarbor Plain contains evidence that Aborigines were painting on its walls at this time. If this dating is accurate, it means that Australian Aborigines were expressing themselves artistically 5000 years before Europe's ancestors had crept into caves in southern France and Spain to begin painting their walls.

Above: Ernest Giles traversed some of Western Australia's most inhospitable deserts and added greatly to the understanding of central Australia.

Opposite: The first European settlement of Western Australia was at Albany in 1826. It was an attempt to discourage the French from claiming the region.

Previous pages: Purnululu (Bungle Bungle) National Park, is renowned for the Beehives—sandstone rock formations with black bands of lichen.

Above: Augustus Gregory (1819–1905), with his brothers Henry and F.T. Gregory, explored north and east of Perth and through the Murchison and Gascoyne regions of Western Australia.

TAMING THE LAND

By 1788 there were about 5000 Aborigines living in the south-western corner of Western Australia. At this time, the great problem for all Aborigines, and subsequently for all Europeans who settled in Western Australia, was the scarcity of water. Although the state covers nearly one-third of the entire Australian continent (it is 2 525 500 square kilometres), most of it is harsh, uninhabitable desert.

The European history of the state has been a continuous battle against the harshness of the vast deserts. Discoveries of great wealth have always been tempered by the harshness of the conditions. It is for this reason that one of the state's heroes is engineer Charles Yelverton O'Connor. His major projects included the state's railways; the establishment of Fremantle harbour; and on the goldfields, the construction of the 563-kilometre water pipeline from Mundaring to Coolgardie and Kalgoorlie. Even though O'Connor and his idea of the pipeline suffered imposing governmental and public opposition, it was completed in 1903, providing vast areas of the wheatbelt and the Eastern Goldfields, which had been depending on unreliable wells, waterholes and condensers, with regular supplies of water. The pipeline assured the survival of Kalgoorlie and Boulder.

EXPLORATION AND EUROPEAN SETTLEMENT

The overwhelming dryness of the region prevented any real European interest in settlement until the early 1800s, when French exploration of the Western Australian coastline combined with the British wars against Napoleon persuaded the London Colonial Office that the region should be settled to prevent French claims on the continent.

Thus in 1826, the New South Wales Governor, Ralph Darling, was instructed to establish a colony at King George Sound with a view to creating a permanent penal colony in the area. The resulting 'penal colony', however, was short lived.

The founding father of modern Western Australia was Captain James Stirling who, in 1827, explored the Swan River area in the HMS *Success*. As a result of his explorations, attempts to establish a new colony in the west were renewed and on 2 May 1829 Captain Charles Fremantle claimed Western Australia for Britain. A month later a party of free settlers, accompanied by free workers (the plan was to establish the colony without convict labour) arrived. Conflict between Aborigines and settlers was immediate. In 1830, Thomas Peel, an early West Australian entrepreneur, established a settlement at the mouth of the Murray and by 1834 it was known that the area around Pinjarra, located 86 kilometres

south of Perth on the banks of the Murray River, it was very fertile. But this settlement met with strong resistance from Aborigines resulting in the infamous Battle of Pinjarra in 1834, one of the most notorious massacres of Aborigines in Australian history.

Fear of reprisals resulted in the fortification of the settlement at Pinjarra. However, the difficulties of clearing the land and growing crops were so great that by 1850 the population had only reached 5886.

In spite of its relative autonomous success, the colony could not resist the temptation of convict labour and on 1 June 1850 the first boatload of convicts arrived. Western Australia became a convict state at a time when the eastern states, largely due to the gold rushes, were abandoning convict labour. Between 1850 and 1868, when the transportation stopped, a total of 9718 convicts had arrived. Their effect on the colony's economy was considerable and by 1869 the population had increased to 22 915.

Serious exploration of the state started in the late 1830s and for the next 20 years men like Major Peter Egerton Warburton, Septimus Roe, the brothers Augustus and Francis Thomas Gregory, and Ernest Giles discovered that most of the state was dry, unforgiving desert. Not surprisingly, these early explorers were not followed by graziers or developers.

Above: It is a comment on the early European settlement of Fremantle that the first building was a gaol. It was, in the early years, the port and administrative centre of the vast colony.

Above: The Pilbara was sparsely settled until the 1880s when gold was discovered at Marble Bar and Nullagine.

GOLD FEVER

It was only in the 1880s, when gold was discovered and prospectors by the tens of thousands swarmed across the land, that any real development of Western Australia occurred. The discovery in the far north in the Kimberley presented major problems of access and transportation. The prospectors weren't dissuaded, however, and gold was subsequently found in the Pilbara and in the Ashburton and Murchison areas.

But it was Paddy Hannan's discovery at Kalgoorlie and the early discoveries at Coolgardie that sparked true gold fever. In 1885, the population of Western Australia was a little over 30 000 and by 1904 it had escalated to 239 000.

WOOL AND WHEAT

The wealth generated from gold soon disappeared and by the early years of the twentieth century the economy was again dependent on wool and wheat. Because of this dependency, the dramatic fall in wool and wheat prices in the late 1920s to early 1930s resulted in the collapse of the state's economy. During this time, the state, partly because of its isolation and partly because the economy was driven by pastoralists, developed a reputation for maltreatment of the indigenous population. The treatment of Aboriginal stockmen on the outback properties was feudal and oppressive and, for a time in the 1930s, there was a strong secession movement. Many West Australians at the time felt that they were far removed from the attitudes and values of the country's eastern states. In 1933, a referendum was held and West Australians voted by a majority of two to one to secede from the rest of the country. Only constitutional problems prevented the split.

By the 1950s, however, thoughts of secession had disappeared as the state, once again, rode to prosperity 'on the sheep's back'.

Above: From the coast spreading east to the goldfields, Western Australia is a vast agricultural land of wheat and sheep.

Following pages: The Pinnacles, located in the Nambung National Park, has over 150 000 calcified limestone pillars.

DEVELOPMENT OF THE STATE

The state's economy did not recover until the post-war federal immigration policy brought a huge influx of migrants, nearly all of them from Britain, to Western Australia during 1947 to 1970. Symbolic of these new immigrants was a child born in London on 22 April 1938—the famous 1980s entrepreneur Alan Bond.

Bond had a passion for Western Australia. He drew worldwide attention to the state by winning the elusive America's Cup, a yachting trophy, and bringing it to Fremantle. He had four attempts at the Cup before success in 1983 with John Bertrand's crew on *Australia II*.

By the mid-1980s, the state was at the height of its reputation as the land of the 'get rich quick'. Entrepreneurs such as Alan Bond, Robert Holmes à Court, Laurie Connell, Brian Burke and others made Western Australia seem like a state of endless opportunity.

In tandem with their remarkable dealings the premier, Brian Burke, did everything in his power to nurture the entrepreneurs. Such was the government's involvement that the term 'W.A. Inc.' was coined to describe its entrepreneurial enthusiasm.

The 1987 Australian stockmarket crash, however, ended many of the entrepreneurs' 'get rich quick' schemes. Holmes à Court lost many, many millions of dollars—as did Australian taxpayers when it was revealed, for example, that millions of dollars were lost in the attempt to prop up the collapsing Rothwells merchant bank.

Above: One of the great yachting destinations in the world: Fremantle Harbour. It was from here that Australia launched its successful challenge for the elusive America's Cup in 1983.

Opposite: The high rise of Perth's central business district is captivating when viewed from Kings Hill.

Above: The coast around Kalbarri offers some of Australia's most beautiful scenery. The red cliffs are a reminder that this is iron-rich country. Further north these red cliffs become the iron mines of the Pilbara region.

Opposite: El Questro Gorge, a reminder that in a state of vast deserts the area known as The Kimberley has pockets of tropical rainforest.

WESTERN AUSTRALIA TODAY

Western Australia's economy is driven by mining, wool and wheat, and yet only 15 per cent of its population live in rural areas. Similarly, it has a population of less than two million and more than 50 per cent of them live in Perth. Perth is probably the only Australian capital city which is almost totally dependent on the economic wellbeing of the whole state.

Western Australia's economy has always been largely dependent on its extraordinary mineral wealth and the vagaries of international wool and wheat prices. To avert such dependence, as early as 1955–56, the area south of Perth known as Kwinana became the site for an oil refinery and a steel mill.

Extensive oil exploration along the state's northern coastline during the 1960s supplemented its industrial base. But the most important event during this period was the discovery of iron ore in the Pilbara region. By any definition this was a huge find, establishing mining towns like Shay Gap, Mount Tom Price, Paraburdoo, Mount Whaleback and Pannawonica. In 1983 vast diamond deposits were found at Lake Argyle in the far north-east of the state. Significant deposits of both alumina and nickel were also found.

Above: Lake Argyle, Australia's largest lake, was built to provide water to the north-east region of the Kimberley.

Opposite: Rain brings superb colour to the vast inland wastelands. Overnight dry dunes are covered in wildflowers.

It is no accident that the state has become known as 'the wild west'. With most of the people living in the Perth–Fremantle area, a feeling remains that life beyond the city in mining camps and on vast cattle properties is one of hardship and isolation. There is still a 'beyond the law' mentality that pervades much of the outback in this vast state. Today Western Australia is a thriving and popular tourist destination, with culturally diverse cities and natural wonders laden with the treasures of time and art. It is a huge source of minerals, with gigantic world-class deposits of iron ore, gold and diamonds.

NORTHERN TERRITORY

THE TOP END

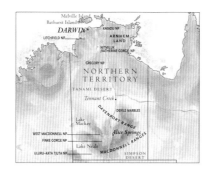

THE TOP END

The Northern Territory is Australia's 'last frontier'. It covers 1 346 200 square kilometres, an area larger than France, Germany and the United Kingdom combined, and yet it has a population of less than 200 000 people, making it smaller than some of Australia's larger towns and cities. It is this contradiction that lies at the heart of this complex region, which aspires to full statehood. Quite different from the rest of Australia, it is really nothing more than a collection of four average-sized towns (Darwin, Alice Springs, Tennant Creek and Katherine) and about 40 tiny outposts. Geographically, this huge area, with a coastline that stretches for 6200 kilometres, ranges from steaming, tropical mangrove swamps through to savanna grassland, scrub and eventually vast tracks of unforgiving desert.

Around Alice Springs is 'the Red Centre', an area of spectacular beauty notable for Uluru (formerly Ayers Rock) and Kata Tjuta (formerly the Olgas), which rise out of the flat wastelands of the desert to mesmerise travellers with their changing colours and their strange, haunting spirituality.

The MacDonnell Ranges sprawl out to the east and the west of 'the Alice'. They are starkly denuded. Here the 'bare bones' of the earth, rising up in jagged, blood-red cliffs, stand out against the cobalt blue of the desert skies and the powerful, haunting white of the ghost gums which abound in the region.

DISCOVERY AND COASTAL EXPLORATION

The first Aborigines arrived in the Northern Territory about 60 000 years ago. They were hunters and gatherers, believed to have travelled across the Indonesian archipelago at a time

Above: In 1824, Captain J.J. Gordon Bremer arrived in Port Essington to establish a settlement. Finding no water his party moved to Melville Island where the settlement lasted four years.

Opposite: Early Darwin was a wild colonial port where drifters from all over the world arrived on ships from exotic destinations.

Previous pages: Kakadu National Park has an incredible assortment of flora and fauna amongst its river systems.

Above: In 1845–46 Ludwig Leichhardt walked 4800 kilometres from southern Queensland across the Great Artesian Basin to the tiny colonial outpost of Port Essington.

when the sea level was much lower than it is today, so that all journeys were either on foot or by canoe and raft with the next island clearly in view on the horizon.

It is now known that fleets of boats manned by Macassans (Indonesian fishermen) have been moving between Australia and the Indonesian archipelago for many thousands of years in this way, regularly making contact and trading with coastal Aborigines.

On the basis of recent evidence it seems that the first non-Aboriginal, non-Macassan to reach the coastline of the Northern Territory was the Chinese explorer Cheng Ho who, in the early years of the fifteenth century, ventured into the Indian Ocean. A statue found near the present-day site of Darwin in 1879 is believed to have been left by him.

Given the proximity of the Dutch trading port of Batavia it is not surprising that the first confirmed European contact with Australia occurred when Willem Janszoon explored Cape York in 1606. Seventeen years later, Jan Carstensz, commanding the Dutch East India ships, the *Pera* and *Arnhem*, sailing east from Batavia, explored the south coast of Papua New Guinea and discovered and named the Gulf of Carpentaria and Arnhem Land. He was the first European to travel along the coast of the Northern Territory.

The entire coastline of the Northern Territory was charted by Abel Tasman in 1644. In 1803, while circumnavigating Australia, Matthew Flinders also charted the coast, although he did not recognise Melville Island as being separate from the mainland—that was discovered by Phillip Parker King in 1818. King was surprised to find that the Aborigines knew some Portuguese, suggesting that they had made contact with Portuguese sailors.

FIRST EUROPEAN SETTLEMENT ATTEMPTS

By the early years of the nineteenth century, the British decided to set up an outpost on the coast of the Northern Territory to protect it from a perceived French threat.

The first attempt at settlement occurred in 1824 when the British government sent three vessels, under the leadership of Captain James John Gordon Bremer, to Port Essington. So determined were they to lay claim to the continent's north coast that all land from 129 to 135 degrees east was declared a British colony. On 26 September 1824 the party landed at King Cove and over the next month a settlement was built. On 21 October it was named Fort Dundas. However, the area was virtually uninhabitable by Europeans because of tropical diseases, extremes of temperature and climate, and the lack of fertile land to grow food. The local Aborigines resisted the settlement and, together with their constant attacks, the attacks of Macassan pirates, and sickness which raged through the settlement, the community was wound down by 1826 and officially closed in 1829.

Far removed from the inhospitable local environment, the bureaucrats in the Colonial Office in London persisted with plans to populate the area with Britons. As reports of the sheer awfulness of life at Fort Dundas filtered through to London, plans were drawn up to establish a second military outpost at Raffles Bay. On 19 May 1827, Captain James Stirling was despatched from Sydney, subsequently establishing Fort Wellington. The crew consisted of some convicts and some members of the 39th Regiment. The settlement suffered the same problems as Fort Dundas of disease, pestilence, tropical lethargy, attacks by Aborigines and isolation, and was closed down in 1829.

Port Essington was the third attempt to settle on the northern coastline. Because the settlement lasted for over a decade, and because it was the site of Ludwig Leichhardt's greatest triumph (crossing north Australia from southern Queensland to Port Essington), it is perhaps more widely known than Raffles Bay and Fort Dundas.

On 26 October 1838, Captain James John Gordon Bremer arrived at Port Essington to set up a military outpost; however, in June 1839, Bremer was posted to China and never returned to the settlement, which was smitten with fever and the problems that had beset the other settlements in the area. Port Essington was abandoned in 1849, and it wasn't until 20 years later that, for several reasons other than being a military site, the successful settlement at Palmerston (the modern day site of Darwin) was established.

Above: Port Essington, the site of the first mainland settlement of the Northern Territory by Europeans was short-lived. The heat and conditions were too harsh for permanent settlement.

Above: The Overland Telegraph Line connected Australia to the rest of the world on Thursday August 22, 1872. Today the Overland Telegraph Station in Alice Springs is a popular tourist attraction.

Opposite: The vast inland of Australia is a desert country characterised by spinifex, low-lying bushes and trees and dry creek beds. This dramatic landscape in the Finke Gorge National Park is typical of much of the Northern Territory.

INLAND EXPLORATION

The Northern Territory's first 'inland' explorers were Ludwig Leichhardt, who journeyed overland from Queensland in 1844, and Augustus Gregory, who trekked south and east from the Victoria River in 1855. As happened all over Australia, these so-called 'explorations' were watched and assisted by Aborigines.

It was partly as a result of the rather exaggerated reports of Leichhardt and Gregory that the interior of the Northern Territory was settled. Both explorers had returned with glowing reports of the grazing potential and this was enough to encourage adventurers to overland cattle into the area in the hope of making a quick fortune.

However, it was really the establishment of the Overland Telegraph Line that opened up the Territory. In fact, it is fair to say that, with the exception of the failed ports along the coast, the history of permanent white settlement in the Territory really started after 1861–62 when John McDouall Stuart crossed the country from south to north.

Stuart's route across the continent subsequently became the route for the Overland Telegraph Line. It was actually worked out using Stuart's maps and journals. The telegraphic repeater stations, which were established at Port Darwin, Yam Creek (Pine Creek), Daly Waters, Powells Creek, Tennant Creek, Barrow Creek, Alice Springs and Charlotte Waters (all of which had reliable water) along the Overland Telegraph route, became the first communities in the Territory. The pastoralists encouraged this development by using the Telegraph Line as a stock route. Later, minerals were discovered.

Right: Vast properties covering hundreds of square kilometres mean that jackaroos have to hunt down the cattle for branding and sending to the markets.

RENEWED SETTLEMENT

In 1863 the entire Northern Territory was annexed to South Australia. On 28 June 1864, the soldier, surveyor and former member of parliament, Boyle Travers Finniss became the governor resident in the Northern Territory. Against commonsense and the advice of his juniors, Finniss chose an area of mosquito-infested mud flats near Escape Cliffs. The decision

was disastrous. He fought with his officials and was disliked by the 80 settlers who had accompanied him, so eventually 30 of the settlers departed to Western Australia. The settlement was abandoned on 11 January 1867. The determination to settle the Territory, however, remained undiminished. In 1869, George Goyder, the Surveyor-General of South Australia, arrived at Port Darwin. By 23 February, he had surveyed the site of Darwin, which was known as Palmerston. The timing was right for settlement. The Overland Telegraph had opened up the inland and by 1874 Palmerston had a population of 600 Europeans and 180 Chinese and Malays. The town had its own newspaper and 11 stores.

By the 1880s, the northern coast was sparsely settled but, like so much of the Territory, all that was required was a severe drought to drive even the most committed pastoralist back to the milder and easier climates of the southern states. The Barkly Tablelands to the south of Darwin were opened up by the famous stockman Nat Buchanan, who travelled from Rocklands Station in Queensland across the Tablelands to the Overland Telegraph Line in 1877. The trip was not hugely successful because, by the time Buchanan arrived at the Telegraph Line, speculators had already claimed, sight unseen, most of the land on the Tablelands. The resulting invasion of sheep led to surveys being carried out in 1879 to determine ownership. In the 1890s, the area became legendary as great herds of beef cattle were driven across the semi-desert areas from the fertile Kimberley into north Queensland. Even today, cattle are still the primary agricultural product in this area, which stretches from the Atherton Tablelands in Queensland to the far northern region of Western Australia.

Conflicts between Aborigines and Europeans were commonplace and the Territory has the distinction of being the last place of a major massacre in Australia, when in 1928 an estimated 17 Aborigines were killed on Coniston Station by a posse lead by the local policeman.

Above: The history of the Northern Territory's cattle industry cannot be told without acknowledging the importance of the Aboriginal stockmen.

Above: A symbol of Darwin's colonial heritage is the beautiful wooden Government House which stands on the shores of Darwin Harbour surrounded by palm trees and tropical gardens.

SEARCH FOR INDEPENDENCE

Independence for the Territory came slowly. In 1890 it elected two members to the South Australian House of Assembly and, with Federation, the Territory became part of the huge electorate of Grey and was able to vote in Commonwealth government elections. In 1911 the Commonwealth government took over the administration of the Territory. It was around this time that Palmerston became known as Darwin. The problems of independence occurred almost immediately when in 1918, angry Territorians marched on Government House in Darwin demanding representation. A subsequent inquiry showed that the Territory had no effective administration. Elections were held in 1922 for a Northern Territory member to the Commonwealth House of Representatives. In 1926, the Territory was split into Central and Northern Australia, but by 1931 it was re-united and once again under the control of an Administrator. These problems continued to drag on until 1 July 1978, when the Territory was granted full self-government. Today the Northern Territory still exists in a rather awkward limbo between 'territory' and 'state'. At the elections in 1998, the residents decided against statehood, which seemed like an extraordinary decision given that, during the previous 12 months, the Territory's legislative integrity was overruled by federal parliament when it passed its Anti-Euthanasia Bill expressly to accede the Northern Territory's Rights of the Terminally Ill Bill, allowing euthanasia in limited circumstances.

MODERN DEVELOPMENT

The view of the Northern Territory as a wild, tropical outpost changed during World War II when fears of a possible Japanese invasion saw it become the front line of Australian defence. Women and children were evacuated from Darwin and early in 1942 a number of American troops joined Australian forces. On 19 February 1942, 188 Japanese aircraft attacked Darwin killing 243 people and wounding approximately 350. Between 19 February 1942 and 12 November 1943, Darwin sustained 64 air attacks resulting in 261 deaths and 410 injured. It was impossible for people in the rest of Australia to pretend that the Northern Territory was a distant outpost. If Darwin was attacked, Australia was being attacked. After the war, the Commonwealth government drew up plans to redevelop Darwin. The rebuilding of the city started in the early 1950s and by the mid-1970s it was expanding rapidly. This progress was halted in 1974 by Cyclone Tracy.

Cyclone Tracy was first located at 9 a.m. on 20 December, 700 kilometres north-east of Darwin. But it didn't stay there—it struck Darwin at 4.15 a.m. on Christmas morning and experts later estimated that the winds had reached 250 kilometres per hour.

It was estimated that the damage bill was in excess of $1000 million. During the seven days that followed the event, 35 362 people were evacuated from the city. Today Darwin is a 'new' city—especially designed to withstand future cyclones.

Above: Today Darwin is an important modern port exporting Australian produce to the huge Asian market which lies to the north.

Following pages: Uluru, Australia's most well-known landmark, is also the world's largest monolith and an Aboriginal sacred site.

ABORIGINAL RIGHTS

Of all the areas in Australia, the Northern Territory has a large number of Aborigines still living traditional lifestyles. Historically, the entire area was settled by Europeans who used the Aborigines as cheap labour and took the land with little thought for the rights of the traditional owners. Some areas, however, have been remarkably lucky. The area around Uluru has fortunately escaped white exploitation. In the early 1900s, the South Australian, West Australian and Northern Territory governments declared the area around the rock a reserve for Aboriginal people. In the 1920s and 1930s, pastoralists tried to assert their dominance over the land. The size of the original reserve was reduced but the grazing of land was short lived. In 1964 pastoral subsidies were revoked forcing Europeans off the land. In the early 1980s, Prime Minister Hawke declared the government's intention to grant inalienable freehold title to the traditional owners and on 26 October 1985 the Governor General, Sir Ninian Stephen, handed the land over to the newly formed Uluru/Kata Tjuta Land Trust.

Other areas have had a much more unhappy history. In 1966, 200 Gurindji stockmen walked off Wave Hill Station protesting over the pay and conditions offered by the giant British company Vesteys. This is seen as the beginning of the modern land rights movement and it culminated in 1975 when the Commonwealth Labor government, having asked the Gurindji to identify their traditional lands, returned 3237 square kilometres on leasehold title.

Today large areas of the Northern Territory belong to the indigenous people. By 1993, nearly 40 per cent of the Territory was under the control of local Aboriginal communities.

Above: Kata Tjuta, 36 domes rising 546 metres from the desert floor, are easily visible on the horizon from Uluru and share the same geological history as the great rock.

Opposite: Uluru—'The greatest stone on Earth' rises from the flat plains which surround it. The base is pockmarked with caves carved by the desert's erosive forces.

Above: Alice Springs. As the sun sinks the desert skyline around Alice Springs turns slowly red before succumbing to the pristine darkness of the desert night.

Opposite: In the dry season Kakadu is, as one critic observed, little more than 'clapped out buffalo country'. In The Wet it comes alive with waterfalls, wetlands and wildlife.

IMPORTANCE OF TOURISM

Even though historically visitors were reluctant to stay in the Northern Territory, it is now one of Australia's premier tourist destinations. The beauties of the Kakadu National Park, the magic of Aboriginal sacred site Uluru and the dry, dramatic scenery around Alice Springs attract vast numbers of visitors to the region.

The challenges of tourism in the Northern Territory are complex, beginning with the climate. There are two dominant kinds of climate—monsoonal at the Top End, and desert from the Barkly Tablelands to the South Australian border.

The monsoon, commonly known as 'The Wet', occurs from late October to March and is characterised by hot humid days which culminate in heavy afternoon storms. During this time, the dirt roads in the Top End are effectively closed, even many of the roads in Kakadu and Litchfield National Parks. The only way to see Kakadu's spectacular Jim Jim Falls in The Wet is by helicopter or plane.

Still, despite these problems, people flock to the area because there is simply nothing quite like Uluru, Kata Tjuta and the Devils Marbles anywhere else in Australia, and Kakadu National Park and Litchfield Park are wonderlands when the lakes and rivers are full and when there is enough water tumbling over the falls.

INDEX